About the Author

Ian MacCabe, born in France in 1934 of a Scottish father and a French mother, moved to England in 1938 with his family due to the impending German invasion. He worked in an insurance company and then took up accounting. He moved to France in 1958 and worked with British auditors before joining IBM European HQ in Paris and after eight years left to become a financial director in different international corporations. Upon retirement, he did research on his parents' origins and their careers, making use of important family archives that he inherited in order to write this book. He is currently translating this book into French. He occasionally writes some poetry as an amusement.

The beautiful hand drawn sketches that make up the cover were created by the author's mother, Jeanne Gastal.

To Professor William Knox,
with my best wishes
Ian MacCabe.

Dedication

I dedicate this book to those working for world peace and in the first instance to peace and unity in Europe, as well as to the educators to assist today's youth to seek to know and understand better the people from other lands than their own and to explain lessons drawn from history.

Ian MacCabe

MY FATHER A SCOT, MY MOTHER FRENCH

(Before and after two World Wars)

AUSTIN MACAULEY PUBLISHERS™

LONDON · CAMBRIDGE · NEW YORK · SHARJAH

A CIP catalogue record for this title is available from the British Library.

ISBN 9781528982092 (Paperback)
ISBN 9781528982108 (ePub e-book)

www.austinmacauley.com

First Published (2020)
Austin Macauley Publishers Ltd
25 Canada Square
Canary Wharf
London
E14 5LQ

Acknowledgments

I wish to mention the amenities and helpful assistance provided by the organisations and staff of The National Library of Scotland, The Mitchell Library of Glasgow, The Registrars in Glasgow and Edinburgh, The Edinburgh Castle Museum Library, The Highland Light Infantry Museum, The National Archives at Kew, The Imperial War Museum, The British Library, The Brighton and Hove Libraries. I am also indebted to Professor William Knox of St Andrews University for his essay that enlightened me on the social and economic evolution of Scotland in the 19th century of which my paternal great- grand parents from Ireland were truly living examples at that time.

Table Of Contents

Synopsis

This book depicts the origins of our two European families, (Scottish/Irish and French/Swiss) both affected by the great war of 1914–1918 and the events that followed. It is not an autobiography, but it expresses what I witnessed, my observations and my research results. It also explains how destiny provided me with a double culture.

Based on extensive research I undertook in Scotland and England, I have reconstructed my father's family origins, and I have made a summary of the Scottish economic and social development as from the middle of the 19th century and described the environment of Nick's earlier years before giving full details of his involvement in the First World War and his subsequent career and family life.

There were nine children in each of my parents' families. My father, Dominic, known as "Nick" in the family, was a Catholic, my mother, Jeanne, was a Protestant, but religion was never a problem in the house. My paternal great grandfather came from Ireland in the middle of the nineteenth century at the time of famine and extreme poverty for the people in order to work in the Lanarkshire coalmines. Two generations later, my father began as an apprentice at the age of 14 in the Clydebank shipyards. The history of the family corresponds exactly to the general evolution included in the description of the social and economic environment of Scotland in the nineteenth century.

At the age of 19, Nick volunteered for the HLI (Highland Light Infantry Regiment) in August 1914. He fought in the Dardanelles in 1915 (July to October). Having found his battalion's company, I have been able to trace and describe in detail the events involving him through the campaign's official War Diaries and other research. Dysentery led to his return to Scotland for treatment in Edinburgh until the latter part of 1916. Nick left an interesting set of poems, drawings and photos collected essentially from his fellow soldier patients and nurses from October 1915 until the autumn of 1916. On January 2, 1917, he was sent to fight in the Somme and I have detailed the official military movements and conditions in which he was involved. In March 1917, his injuries sent him back to the UK and demobilisation in April 1918. His elder brother, Peter, had enrolled in the King's Own Liverpool Regiment and was killed at Ypres on November 16, 1914.

As for my mother, Jeanne, her grandfather, Jules Jacques Combe was Swiss and had spent 18 months at Heidelberg as Tutor for the children of the Grand Duke Heritor of Saxony. I show a testimonial and a letter in later years from the Grand Duke. In Belgium, Jules set up a printing company and worked also as a translator French/English/German. Later, he settled in Nanterre, France, where his daughter Juliette, who had married a Frenchman, gave birth to nine children, my mother Jeanne being the eldest. Jules Jacques Combe translated into French and published the French version of Andrew Carnegie's book "The Triumph of Democracy"; he also wrote stories for the children of the family and long and interesting letters to his unmarried daughter, Jeanne Jacqueline (my mother's "Tante Jeanne"). He also had a great interest in scientific matters. For this reason, I have brought to light some of his achievements based on original documents I possess.

In the early part of the 1914–1918 War, Jeanne was a "gouvernante" (an au-pair girl) for a family in Bristol. Her eldest brother, Edouard "Doudou", a wood sculptor at the École Boulle (a famous art school in Paris), was killed on March 25, 1918, in the Somme battle. I possess many of his moving handwritten letters with envelopes sent from the trenches to his mother and family up until three days before his death. His name figures on the Nanterre war memorial as well as on that of his former art school. It is interesting to see the official documents and how the French administration treated the question of soldiers killed in action.

After demobilisation in 1918, Nick joined the large Singer factory at Clydebank, went to night school and became a textile engineer. He settled in France in 1920 working for an American textile company, travelling all over Europe and the Middle East until 1938. Nick met Jeanne in Nanterre, and they married in 1921. Their first child, Peter, was born in November 1922. In 1925, his brother, Douglas, was born. Tragically, in 1930, on March 24, Peter died of meningitis at the age of seven. By coincidence, I was born in 1934 on the same day, March 24. During the inter-war period, Nick was constantly travelling in Europe and the Middle East in conditions quite different to those of today. There are good photo souvenirs of family summer holidays spent in Normandy.

The darkening clouds menacing war spread from Germany to the rest of Europe and from what Nick himself witnessed in Germany, led to a great extent to Nick's decision in 1937 to return to Britain; we finally did in September 1938. After arrival in the UK, there was with former colleagues of the company, an exchange of a few enlightening letters about the drama that was taking place in the period just prior to the outbreak of the Second World War.

In the Second World War, Nick participated actively in the local civil defence system in Brighton as an Air Raid Warden. My brother Douglas was eight years older than me and at 17, he faked his age to join the Royal Navy serving in the naval convoys to Russia. Aboard the "HMS Belfast", he was involved in the battle with the German battleship Scharnhorst that was sunk on December 26, 1943, an event that I have described in this book.

I have also related our daily life and particular events in Brighton during the war and after in peacetime. During these periods, Nick's health gradually deteriorated, certainly partly due to the 1914–18 War plus extensive travelling in his career, then a duodenal ulcer and later lung cancer. A few weeks after I had completed two years National Service in the army (RASC), he died on July 19, 1954 at the age of 59.

There is, unfortunately, not enough material available to satisfy my total curiosity and interest in my father's life and thoughts, although I still have a clear recollection of some of our talks and his remarks, which as the years have passed, I consider them now to have been too few. However, with some effort on my memory, I have given a faithful account of what I remember in our conversations. I have undertaken this research not only in order to collect facts, but also as a tribute to the memory of Nick and Jeanne and at the same time to inform their descendants who really have little intimate knowledge of the family background. The history of Jeanne and her family contains much that is worth bringing to light from a cultural and social point of view. It was concurrent to that of Nick's family, and the simultaneous events in Europe provide great interest and I have thus deemed it essential to put together all that information with the interesting historical archives that I have inherited and also gathered up from all quarters. Today, it shows how much the world has changed since then and at the same time that power struggles continue!

I must mention that some of the numerous archives have been put in the annex to maintain better visibility of the text, and also because there are long interesting letters in French that may not be of interest for readers and for whom I have made comments with translations in certain cases. This account, with its horrors of war, is today a reminder of how precious it is to ensure peace, but of course not at any price, as the lesson of the Second World War teaches us! I have written it in English and I am, at present, translating it into a French version as well.

The final year of the centenary of the First World War has recently passed. It appears to me to be not too late, in the interest of survivors of the Second World War and for families whose ancestors were involved in the First World War, as well as for the general public, to bring to light any additional information on the events that affected so many lives in Europe before these souvenirs begin to fade away. My father's album of photos as well as compiling written contributions by his fellow comrades in convalescence in 1916 shows names and faces that may be identified in other peoples' family souvenirs.

Preface

This book is not an autobiography but an account of the lives of my two European families of mixed origins and different backgrounds at the end of the 19th century and during the 20th century. This period was particularly marked by two world wars in which their members, like those of so many other families from different parts of the world, were directly involved and affected by the tragedy of losing parents and friends. Different European brothers in arms, such as Scots and French, defended together basic human values. My study of archives and what I experienced and learned from conversations and factual evidence enabled me to reconstruct events that our families lived through in days of peace as well as in times of war. They also reveal the cultural differences between French and British in the way of expressing thoughts and feelings and in the general way of living. Throughout my life, this dual culture has been a blessing for me personally and professionally.

I decided to do this research not only in order to satisfy my own curiosity, but also because I consider that I owe it to the memory of my Scottish father Dominic, called "Nick" and my French mother, "Jeanne", as well as their respective families, and also to pass this on to their descendants who today really have little intimate knowledge of the family background. Jeanne's life and her family history contain much that is worth bringing to light. It was concurrent to that of Nick, and it seems to me that a comparison of simultaneous events in Europe is of great interest, even outside of the family circle, and I deem it essential to put together all that knowledge with the historical archives which I have gathered up from all quarters, however limited they may be. Today, the world has much changed since then, but not power struggles nor armed conflicts.

Of course, I regret not having initiated this work earlier in my life when certain people still alive then could have given me more information and clarification on events that I can no longer obtain. When we met, we tended to discuss day-to-day matters rather than to delve into the past. In looking back, I also realise that certain documents and letters escaped my control and have disappeared forever. However, that's life because at different times, we don't always see the priorities in the same order, as we may do later on, but I am nevertheless pleased to have attempted to undertake this exercise and I consider that it's better late than never!

Chapter I
Social and Economic Background
of Scotland in the 19th Century

The life of my ancestors on Nick's side in the middle of the nineteenth century represents the perfect example of the history of Scottish social and economic development of that period and later that researchers brought to light.

The main Scottish industry in the early 19th century was textiles situated in the proximity of water used as energy. The situation in Scotland around 1840 was such that more than half of the population lived and worked on the land or in small industrial villages earning their keep from handloom weaving. In the countryside, Scots were generally highly religious and well-educated in socially mixed parish schools, but due to the enclave of their geographical situation, their lifestyle was rather a narrow and insular one, but nevertheless of a tolerable standard. However, it was very different in the Highlands where people were almost impoverished.

With the growth of the coal industry enabling a new form of energy, the mechanisation of the manufacturing process moved closer to urban areas where manpower could be attracted. In addition, a new industry for Scotland was developed, notably the iron industry that attracted investors. The introduction of mechanised transport, the railway, in 1842, between Glasgow and Edinburgh, was a start for improving communications, the subsequent expansion of which brought benefits to both the coal and iron industries and to the economy in general.

As a result of these changes, migrants from the Highlands and Ireland were attracted to these urban areas looking for work and accommodation. This movement provoked the transformation of agriculture. On one hand there was a need for more food for an increasing urban population while the rural population diminished, and on the other hand, agricultural production required greater efficiency which was obtained by mechanisation with labour saving machinery as well as the introduction of more scientific methods of farming by crop rotation and enclosure. As for accommodation, great social and health problems arose due to the shortage of housing, overcrowding and the lack of adequate sanitary and social structures. At one time between the 1830s and 1840s, only one third of Glasgow's children went to school and it was entirely due to industry's need for child labour despite the passing of the Factory Acts during that period. From 1801 to 1840, the population of Glasgow increased by 220% from 77,000 to 275,000 of which it said that 44,000 were Irish born residents. At Coatbridge, predominantly the homes of coal miners, the Irish born population represented 35.8% of the total in 1851.

Mainly after 1850, the introduction of steel shipbuilding and marine engineering completed the Scottish industrial complex creating a greater demand for a work force as Scotland's economic progress advanced rapidly. The universities of Scotland, compared to England, awarded greater recognition to science and engineering and thus the Scots' inventiveness together with cheap energy supplies as well as iron ore in the western part of the country, work skills and lower wages compared with other areas of Britain, soon gave Scotland an early lead in marine technology and shipbuilding. Scotland also took a lead in the railway industry, notably by manufacturing locomotives in the Springburn district of Glasgow.

From the mid-1800s onwards, the urban authorities acted to confront the major social problems arising from the growing population in the cities, notably housing and disease. The Poor Law (Scotland) Act was passed in 1845 creating parochial boards for building poorhouses (indoor relief) and distributing aid to paupers (outdoor relief). In 1859, Glasgow authorities opened a supply of clean water from Loch Katrine in the Trossachs, followed by Edinburgh which drew water from St Mary's Loch in the Borders, thus effectively minimising epidemics of cholera. In 1860, both cities each appointed medical officers of health setting an example for other large burghs to follow. In 1866, Glasgow introduced a ticketing system to control the numbers living in slum housing and set up the Glasgow Improvement Trust. By 1902, Glasgow Town Council owned 2.488 houses. Schooling was made compulsory for children aged between five and thirteen years old with prosecution for parents when attendance was not regular by passing the Education (Scotland) Act of 1872.

By the end of the 19th century, despite the problems that had accompanied the important economic growth, the increase in wages and many improvements in the standard of living had been brought about. However, the overall economic situation was already changing on the eve of the new century. The cotton industry, with the exception of the thread sector, collapsed in the 1890s unable to compete with the low wages applied in Lancashire. The output of the iron industry fell, as the supply of local iron ore diminished leading to a reduction in Scotland's share of the total British steel output. Imports of iron ore grew steeply at increased costs contributing to a fall in the profit margins of the Clyde shipyards and of other productions requiring steel.

With the slowdown of the economy and a reduction in the work force, as well as the breakdown of the fishing industry in the 1880s, between 1901 and 1910 emigration from Scotland was again on the rise. North America, Australia and South Africa presented greater perspectives than Scotland, and inhabitants from the Lowlands as well as the Highlands plus a great number of crofters[1] took their chances in these countries. During this period, net emigration ran at the equivalent of 52% of the natural increase of the population representing 282,000 people.

Despite increased attention given to the problem of poverty, the amount of money spent to overcome it was far too little and a great deal less than the amount spent in England, which on average was a third more than the amount spent in Scotland on its poor. Women earned much less than men and between the skilled and unskilled worker, there was a large gap. The Islands and the Highlands remained poor, with agricultural wages in 1907 13% below the British average. The infant mortality rate increased during the 19th century reaching 122 per 1,000 live births in the 1904/05 period much above the figures for England and Wales. Bad housing conditions and poverty were mainly responsible. In Glasgow, 32% of the children who died before the age of five in the 1890s lived in one-roomed houses. It must be said that big building projects, private as well public, were underway in Glasgow at the end of the 1800s, such as in the area of Hyndland. Most were one roomed or two roomed due to the financial limitations of the population. Building continued after the First World War on the return of soldiers from their service; in 1934, more than 50% of which was public sector housing.

In Scotland, there were numerous religious institutions, the strength of which lay more in the urban areas, as compared with England, according to the religious census of 1851. In the 1880s, the churches were seen to be more sensitive to the social causes of poverty and began to look into the failings of the market economy. The Glasgow Presbytery's inquiry into housing conditions in the 1890s reflected this attitude just as the founding of the Christian Social Union in the early 1900s. As far as church attendance was concerned, a survey carried out in 1900 indicated that few unskilled workers went to church with a slightly better but still

---

[1] Crofters were tenants of small agricultural landholdings who on coastal areas also lived from their fishing and whose revenues had dropped sharply and were now unable to pay their rents.

low attendance for those of the Catholic Church representing a largely lower working-class population. Catholic Irish families suffered from prejudices of Presbyterian Scotland, as they were looked down upon as being uncivilised, drunken, idle and lazy. Irish Protestant immigrants in the 1870s and 1880s, bringing in their Orange Lodges with them were not treated in the same way. Certain occupations were recruited on a religious basis and such discrimination and prejudices kept the Irish Catholics at the bottom of the heap.

Due to limited public funds, school boards had difficulty developing secondary education. Although educational reforms had widened access at all levels, secondary and higher education mainly profited the middle and upper classes. In 1886, the famous high schools of Glasgow and Edinburgh as well as Perth Academy had no working-class pupils, thus the belief long persisted that only a small talented proportion of children would benefit from further education. In 1901, the school leaving age was increased to 14 and remained unchanged until after the Second World War. The Education act of 1918 brought Roman Catholic schools into the state system, but subsequently, Catholics were generally subject to strong protests and harassment by extremist Protestant organisations until the signs of an oncoming war in the late 1930s helped to calm things down.

At the outbreak of the First World War in August 1914, Scotland remained a country marked by profound inequalities in the distribution of wealth despite the industrial development and the growth of its economy during the preceding half century. The country could not rely on the growth of its domestic market due to poverty and also its reliance on heavy industry was essentially based on the international market but subject to uncontrollable fluctuations in demand. The armaments build up prior to the war gave only temporary relief. The overall situation at that moment, added to patriotic fervour, explains why voluntary military recruitment was proportionately higher in Scotland than elsewhere in Great Britain.

The outcome of the First World War in Scotland was an increased involvement of the state in the economy and social affairs. Due to men volunteering for military service, women then played a role in industry, such as the manufacturing of munitions and taking up posts in the transport services. Rent controls were introduced in 1915 following a rent strike on Clydeside. The government took into temporary ownership munitions factories as well as coalfields and the railways.

Just after the end of the war in 1918, a restocking boom created a provisional period of expansion until the economy was hit by a depression in 1920 that lasted until the rearmament campaign of the latter part of the 1930s. State subsidies ended with the return of industries to private hands that led to fierce competition. Industrial output fell dramatically; shipbuilding production in 1919 of 650,000 tons fell to only 74,000 tons in 1933, while the peak of coal output in 1913 of 42.5m tons fell to an average of 30 m tons between 1919 and 1938, coal exports dropping by 20% between 1913 and 1935. After 1930, many shipyards considered to be obsolete or empty were closed down. Due to these factors and because Scotland had hitherto been committed to heavy industry, its unemployment in 1939 was much higher (16%) than the rest of the UK (11%)[2].

Various schemes and policies were tried with little effect and the situation led many people to emigrate. In the period 1921–1931 Scotland lost 400,000 of its population (8%). In the early 1930s, 25% of the West of Scotland insured workforce was out of work. Unfortunately, in the latter part of the 1930s, many families that had emigrated, especially to go to America, returned home owing to the even more severe economic depression that took place there. The National Insurance Act of 1912 thought to have only a temporary purpose of keeping skilled respectable male workers and their families from falling into the underclass of the Edwardian society, was overwhelmed as from 1920 by the influx of demobilised men, the downturn in the economy and those excluded from national insurance schemes who no longer had rights to benefits. Subsequently, with cost cutting measures, the state did manage to provide welfare to give families a modicum of dignity, and it is noted that in the inter war years there was a decline in infant mortality.

As the economic depression worsened after 1929 and the main churches were losing members, the Protestant Action Society in Edinburgh made important gains in local elections and carried out a policy of attacking and harassing Catholic gatherings. The conflict was also reflected in gang warfare arising out of football matches. Protestants (Billy Boys) backed Glasgow Rangers F.C. while the Catholics (the Norman Congs) supported the Glasgow Celtics F.C. In the late 1930s, however, things died down as the oncoming war loomed up and as Catholics joined the armed forces in the same patriotic spirit as the Protestants.

During the interwar period of economic depression, entertainment in the form of the radio, the cinema and other enjoyments provided cheap forms of distraction, whereas alcohol acted also as a diversion, but created drunkenness with all the associated social problems. As for the rich classes, their investment in hunting activities (deer stalking, fishing

---

[2] The total unemployed in the UK was 1,800,000 per W.W. Knox, A History of the Scottish people.

and shooting) and in the building of expensive hunting lodges brought little to the overall local economy, while the number of shepherds they had previously employed declined.

Overall, although the 1930s witnessed the passing away of an industrial order, the transformation of which clearly produced economic casualties, the poor and the unemployed nevertheless now had entitlement to receive support from society. Without being generous, that support did allow a standard of decency unthinkable in the 1840s and few of the unemployed or poor were evicted or lost their possessions in this latter period.

The Second World War fed Scottish industry for a short while, but after peace in 1945, the Scottish industrial structure was gradually replaced by an economy based on services, light industry and consumer trades leading to an increase in the standard of living for most people in Scotland in the 1950s and 1960s. The coming of the Welfare State helped to better cope with poverty and bad housing, thereby reducing social tensions. Scotland could now look towards the future on a similar footing to that of the rest of Britain and Western Europe.

Chapter II
Origins of Nick's Family

Great-grandfather, Peter McCABE

I recall Nick telling me that his grandfather, of Irish origin from the Catholic part of Belfast, was a coal miner who started working in the pits at the age of 12 and he stressed several times the hard conditions of that life. From parish records, it is indicated that he married Margaret McGaughran on April 10,1853 at Mearns, Renfrewshire. She was also an Irish immigrant. The 1861 census undertaken in Scotland, for N° 17 Main Park Close, in the Parish of Monkland, in the town of Coatbridge, County of Lanark, stated that Peter McCabe, 30 years of age, Coal Miner, lived there with his wife Margaret, also 30 years of age and that both were born in Ireland. Living with them, their three sons: Patrick, 5 years old; Dominick, 3 years old and Edward, 1 year old, all three born in Lanark, Old Monkland were also recorded. The census indicated that of the children between 5 and 15 years of age attending school there were none at that time, and that the number of rooms with one or more windows amounted to one.

In the next census which took place in 1871, Peter McCabe and his family were shown to be living in the same Monkland area at 112 Spittal Row, Buchanan Street, with three additional children, Peter, then 9 years old, Margaret 7 years old and lastly James 3 years old. It is noted therein that Patrick and Dominick, now respectively 13 and 15 years old, were coal miners like their father, whereas Edward and Peter were described as Scholars. In the next census of 1881, Peter and his wife Margaret were living at 35 Buchanan Street with only James, a scholar, and Margaret, now 17, General "Serv" (out of employ), plus a lodger Peter Sharkey from Ireland, a Labourer in Iron Works.

Great-grandfather, Peter McCabe, died in Glasgow on March 22, 1901, at 422 Great Eastern Road, Glasgow, at the age of 63 of "senile decay, and bronchitis, 4 months". The records of his death mention that his father was called Dominick, a labourer and his mother, Dorothy (born McDonagh).

Peter's wife, Margaret, whose maiden name was McGaughran (with different spellings in some of the registered documents), died on March 26, 1909 at the age of 68 at 864 Great Eastern Road, Glasgow. Her father, Edward, was stated to have been a farmer; her mother's maiden name was Flannagan, forename Bridget.

I visited Coatbridge, in the summer of 2007, only to find that the mineworkers' houses had all disappeared from Monkland, the area having been developed into new housing estates eating up at the same time former farmland, as told to me by a very helpful and friendly local man, Archibald, I met on the spot. The old cemetery at Coatbridge however still exists, but I did not have time to go there.

In George Orwell's book "On the road to Wigan Pier", there are several chapters describing the terrible conditions of mining in the 1930s as well as the difficult housing situation during the depression, and in his research he quotes Coatbridge and included a photo of the workmen's houses there (see annexe).

Grandfather Dominick

Peter McCabe's second son, Dominick Snr. was my grandfather, born around 1858. On the 1871 Census, he was shown as being a coal miner; on June 25, 1884, at that moment as a tube work labourer, he married Mary Hart, a Cotton Factory Miller of Scottish descent, in the Sacred Heart Chapel, Bridgeton, Glasgow. Mary's father, Joseph Hart, was a Cotton Spinner (Operative) and her mother, also Mary, M.S. Hughes was not shown as having a profession. At that time, Dominick MacCabe Snr. lived at 637 Dalmarnock Road, Bridgeton.

Nick's parents, Dominick Snr. and Mary

On the birth certificate of his first child, Agnes, born in 1885, Dominick McCabe Snr is mentioned as being a Spirit Dealer's Salesman.

He died on June 25, 1935, the day of the 51st anniversary of his marriage. His wife, Mary, died June 6, 1952. I remember Nick going to Scotland for his mother's funeral where he joined his brother, Joseph, who had remained single and had lived all his life with his mother. Long before, all six daughters had left home, five of them had, for sure, left Scotland.

According to the last published census, that is to say the one that took place in 1911 and which was published in May 2011, it appears that ten children were born "alive", but only a total of nine children "still living" were recorded. No trace of a tenth child appears in the earlier censuses consulted. Of these nine children, six were girls and three were boys[3], as shown below with the year of birth:

Agnes, in 1885; Margaret, 1886; Mary, 1887; Bridget called "Nettie", 1889; Peter, 1891; Elizabeth, 1893; Dominick, my Father, called "Nick" 1895 (later he spelt his name Dominic without the "k"); Dorothy called "Dolla", 1897; Joseph, 1899.

My Father, Dominic ("Nick")

No records of where Nick went to school are yet at hand, but there is, however, simply an undated recommendation from the Naval Chaplain at St Peter's, Partick:

"I have known Dominic McCabe, 11 Airlie Gardens, Partick, for the last ten years. He is a member of my congregation. I have always found him to be a straightforward and manly lad, exemplary in his conduct, robust and enthusiastic in his games and most attentive to his religious duties.

'I can with every confidence recommend him to any position of trust."

Rev Michael McNairney MR (Missionary Rector), Naval Chaplain, North Bank of Clyde[4].

From our conversations, I recall Nick telling me that he began work at the age of 14 as an apprentice at John Brown's Shipyard at Clydebank and that he went to night school.

---

[3] As for information collected on Nick's brothers and sisters, this appears in Chapter VIII devoted to their history.

[4] As this reference is undated, it could have perhaps only served after the War when he postulated for work in France with the Universal Winding Company of Boston

Chapter III
World War I

Enlistment

At the outbreak of the First World War, as a volunteer, like all others, on August 12, 1914 Nick joined the colours of the Highland Light Infantry, a territorial regiment of the city of Glasgow. There is a photo of his HLI group at Gorriemaur on September 25, 1914; these tough young men still have a carefree look of innocence, not yet having faced the horrors of war.

Group of "C" Company 1/5 H.L.I. taken at Gorriemaur Camp September 25.
1914
(My father on the far-left sitting legs apart)

What urged these youngsters to volunteer? Was it a sense of duty and pride for their country, or an answer for youth's thirst for adventure or just an opportunity to get away from the rigours of the daily work routine? As described in the chapter on the social and economic background of those times, the low wages and the slump in the economy are most likely the main reason besides patriotism. Like in all these occasions, there was probably a mixture of all those feelings in deciding to sign up. Whatever the mixed motives, it takes courage to go to war and at the same time, youth does not always sufficiently foresee the realities awaiting them. As the events unfolded, these lads who became men, carried out their duties with bravery and abnegation.

Gallipoli

I narrate here what I recall from different conversations I had with Nick relating to the five months he spent at the Dardanelles front and also from what I gleaned from official archives and books by authors recognised as being competent on the subject retracing the movements of his regiment[5].

First of all, it is useful to recall briefly the background to the war in Turkey, the circumstances in 1914 and the reasons given for the war campaign carried out on Turkish soil. On June 28, 1914, while on a visit to Sarajevo, capital of Bosnia, the Austrian Archduke, Franz Ferdinand and his wife were assassinated. Serbia was suspected of being behind this murder. Different political alliances between countries triggered off preparations for a state of war. On July 28, Austria-Hungary declared war on Serbia prompting Russia to mobilise her southern armies in support of Serbia. In turn, Germany presented an ultimatum to Russia and ordered general mobilisation, as did Russia and Austria also. France was bound by treaty to stand by Russia. This was not the case for Great Britain, but because it, like France and Germany, was one of the guarantors for the neutrality of Belgium, requested Germany assurance that the integrity of Belgium would be respected. The reply from Germany was evasive and on August 3, Germany declared war on France and the next day on Belgium whose frontier was crossed immediately by cavalry followed by infantry that afternoon. On August 4, Great Britain declared war on Germany.

It should be mentioned that there already existed close ties between Germany and Turkey since the latter part of the 19th century that strengthened as the Ottoman Empire began to crumble ("The Sick Man of Europe") because the Germans saw the economic prospects from which they could take advantage by investing in the country. When the 1914 conflict began, the Turks feared the threat of the Russian invasion and were only too glad to get the military support of Germany. The up and coming Young Turks, notably Mustapha Kemal, who looked to bring about changes in the Ottoman Empire were not overjoyed by the German

[5]Oatts, Lt Col L.B., Proud Heritage, The Story of the H.L.I. 1882–1918, ed. Grant; Official History of the War: Military Operations – Morrison. Gallipoli; War Diary of the Gallipoli Campaign in the National Archives at Kew; The Highland Light Infantry 1914–1918 by F.L.
this basic information, it has been made possible to obtain copies of the War Diaries relating the movements and events of the 17th Battalion HLI during the two and a half months fighting in the Somme until March 12, 1917 at which point my father was shipped back to England for medical care.

influence: if Germany were to lose, the Turks would be finished; if Germany won, they would become satellites. However, it was already agreed in 1913 that the Germans would reorganise the Ottoman Army and subsequently it was a German general, Liman von Sanders who commanded the German and Ottoman forces on Gallipoli in 1915. It must be said that despite the Young Turks' misgivings about the political relationship with Germany, from an operational point of view both parties had a great respect for each other's military competence, efforts and courage. Following the German invasion of France, confronted by the French Army and the British Expeditionary Force, by the end of 1914, both sides were entrenched in Northern France in a kind of stalemate. At the end of October 1914, German warships accompanied by a Turkish squadron entered the Black Sea and without warning attacked the Russian port of Odessa and the fortress of Sebastopol and sank all Russian merchant ships nearby.

Taking into account the pressure on the western front, the difficult situation encountered by Russia in the Caucus against Turkey and the attempt by Turkey to seize the Suez Canal and to evict the British from Egypt, which easily failed, the British War Council approved a plan to strike at Constantinople by sending a naval expedition in cooperation with France and Russia. It was hoped also that this operation would distract some of the German forces on the western front and give the Allies some relief. However, several factors made this venture difficult to achieve. To attain Constantinople that lies at the mouth of the Bosphorous by boat, it is necessary to pass through the Dardanelles channel from the Aegean Sea leading to the Sea of Marmara. This channel narrows just before the Marmara Sea and was militarily well-protected from both the European and the Asian sides by artillery installations as well as by a series of mines laid in the water. Also, any boats taking this direction, even if assisted by minesweepers, would find the going quite slow because of the strong current against them due to the effect of the rivers feeding the Black Sea, pouring afterwards through the Bosphorous and then the Sea of Marmara before flowing naturally into the Aegean by way of the Dardanelles.

Naval bombardments in November 1914 were aimed at destroying Turkish defences so that the naval forces could get through the straits of the Dardanelles, but despite the damage that had been inflicted, the British naval attempts in February 1915 to force their way through the channel failed. This was due to the fact that since the attacks in November 1914 by the Navy, the Turks had immediately activated the strengthening of their defences added to the navigational difficulties already mentioned above and anti-submarine netting at Nara Burnu the entry into the Sea of

Marmara leading to Constantinople. A last attempt in March with the ship "Queen Elizabeth" using heavy artillery and causing much damage was finally thwarted by Turkish gunfire and by additional mine laying which resulted in many British and French ships and submarines sinking and leading to the retreat of the remainder of the fleet on March 18.

At the outset of the campaign against Turkey, the project was based on a purely naval expedition and it was not envisaged originally to send troops there. This was partly due to the preoccupation "to killing Germans" on the western front and to avoid further distribution of troops elsewhere. After the failure of the naval expedition, it was finally decided to despatch troops to the Gallipoli Peninsula, on both the European and Asian sides of the Dardanelles to free the blockage. A British Mediterranean Expeditionary Force was formed consisting of the 29th Division, the Royal Naval Division, the 1st Australian Division, the Anzac Division, the 42nd East Lancashire Division and the 29th Indian Infantry Brigade. It was to land on the Gallipoli Peninsula (in Europe) from April 25, 1915 at various points while French troops were to land on the Asiatic side at Kum Kale.

By now, the Turkish defences had been considerably strengthened and their superior position overlooking the narrow strip of landing beaches put the Allies in a weak posture. The landing proved to be difficult and dangerous and by the end of the first three days, very little progress forward was achieved. It became clear that a greater number of troops were required and hence additional forces, notably the Scottish 52nd (Lowland) Division, were shipped in May to Egypt, the British Mediterranean base.

Nick's 1/5th battalion of the H.L.I. within the 52nd (Lowland) Division was part of the 157th H.L.I. brigade in the Mediterranean Expeditionary Force and left Scotland on May 25, 1915 for Devonport, Plymouth where they embarked the next day on the Transylvania for Egypt. The troops landed at Alexandria on June 5, but only for a brief stay before re-embarking and sailing northwards and then back a few days later to Alexandria. From there, they went, most likely for training, to Aboukir in the desert for a couple of weeks where they were subjected to the Khamsin, a hot south or south eastern wind in Egypt blowing at that time of the year. This was one of many unforgettable experiences as Nick related how the sand got into everything like, boots, clothing and food, with flies and other beastly insects as company; it was a situation soon to be repeated after landing at the Gallipoli peninsula.

In the meantime, French troops were also posted on the Gallipoli peninsula, on the right flank of the British forces. (In all the French participation in the operations totalled 80,000 men with about 27,000 casualties, a fact often forgotten.) Between June 4 and June 21, severe combats took place around Krithia where French troops were very active, suffering important losses of 2,500 men in the last attack, but were successful with their 75mm artillery and trench mortars inflicting 5,800 casualties on the Turks. Later, on July 12, they had the occasion to lend important support to the British infantry.

On June 28, the brigade set sail on the Menominee for the Aegean and the Dardanelles. It is recorded that all ranks were in the highest spirits and enjoyed the voyage, singing "Farewell to Aboukir" and making their own music thanks to their individual talents. The boat arrived at the bay of Mudros on July 1, but disembarked July 3 at Cape Helles[6].

According to the official War Diary[7], on July 2 17h00 part of the 157th brigade of the H.L.I. embarked on "T.B. Racoon" and the other part, including "C" Company (Nick's unit) and "D" Company, on the "Whitby Abbey". At 21h30, "T.B. Racoon" moved alongside the destroyer "SS River Clyde" that had already run aground in the bay, and the troops started to disembark by climbing ladders to go on to this ship. It was a dark night with thunderstorm and rain. The men crossed the "SS River Clyde" to the other side of the ship and then, on to pontoons towards the beach, but making slow progress because the pontoons had been damaged by shellfire. Nick's unit "C" as well as Company "D" of the brigade from the minesweeper "Whitby Abbey" landed only the next morning, July 3 at 08h30 and once ashore they pushed onwards to "Rest Trenches" Group I.

---

[6]See in Annex a bird's eye view map of the Gallipoli Peninsula showing the position of the armies on the battlefield. Map Source: Project Gutenberg.
[7]Crown copyright – As recorded in War Diary on July 1, 1915, stored in National Archives at Kew.

A view of "V Beach" taken from S.S. River Clyde[8]

For he who had done his apprenticeship in John Brown's Clydebank Shipyards, as well as his fellow Glaswegian compatriots, what feelings could they have had at that moment when crossing through a ship with the name "River Clyde" now in the same foreign waters as themselves so far from home?

Unlike some of the soldiers of the 29th Division, the 157th brigade of the H.L.I., a territorial force, had no previous fighting experience and were now about to face the realities of war, not just the exposure to gunfire and death but to new daily routines to ensure survival in the heat, dust and dirt, fly ridden air, shortage of drinkable water and lack of variety in the food rations, as well as the outbreaks of disease, all cramped in the limited space of the encampment and trenches. Indeed, the allied forces held a very narrow strip of terrain on the coastline and occupied trenches on the cliff head in front of the Turkish defences. Infantry attacks aimed at investing the Turkish lines were murderously mowed down by machine guns[9]

---

[8]Photo Crown copyright – now in the public domain.
[9] See annex for extracts of the history of the HLI.

GALLIPOLI

BATTLE OF 12TH JULY, 1915

GALLIPOLI battle July 12, 1915

The map made for this battle[10] showing the topology and the military placements, gave familiar British names to locate the different trenches, such as Oxford Street, Regent Street, Leicester Square, etc. War does not preclude the British sense of humour nor being practical.

The two last Companies to arrive, Nick's unit, Company "C" and Company "D" were already subjected to enemy fire and a captain was wounded by shrapnel and sent back immediately to Mudros on the Whitby Abbey. The already depleted 29th Division held the line in front of the newly arrived 52nd Division against whom the Turks launched an attack on July 5. Fought to a standstill, the enemy drew off and the HLI brigade was ordered forward to support and relieve the brigades of the 29th Division and to move into their trenches; Nick's unit was sent to where the Munster Fusiliers were positioned. The War Diary notes on July 7 "intensely hot".

On July 10 and 11, preparations were made for an important attack on the enemy for July 12. His company was ordered to remain in Mercer Street. A remark in the notes indicates that a bomb caused a certain

---

[10] Map Source: Project Gutenberg. This map shows the disposition of the Allied trenches at the time of the battle on July 12, 1915 with popular street name given to identify the different trenches.

amount of *confusion* and congestion, and that the advance ordered at short notice clashed with the movement of battalions. The 5th Bn and the Argyle and Sutherland Highlanders were unable to enter trenches as arranged and the 7th H.L.I. was jammed up in Oxford Street.

At 04h30 on July 12, the bombardment of the enemy trenches commenced. At 07h35, artillery attack by the French and by the 155th brigade launched on the right. At 17h00, brigade attacked and Nick's unit moved forward into Trotman Road. At 18h55, 25 men with tools from his unit were detailed to go to Brigade HQ at Port Arthur. Ten minutes later, orders from the brigade were given to his unit to move forward to support the 7th H.L.I. However, when they arrived, there was no room for them in the captured trenches. There were many movements of the four H.L.I. companies giving support to the 6th and 7th H.L.I. battalions, bringing back prisoners for interrogation and taking over captured trenches. All night officers and men brought ammunition and supplies up to the front line.

The next day more movements for reinforcing the position continued. Several officers were seriously wounded and others killed in action or trying to retrieve 6th battalion machine guns. At 15h40, following a conference at brigade HQ, a Naval Battalion was to attack trenches still occupied by the enemy on the right of the 155th brigade. This occurred at 16h30 and it suffered very heavily in advancing. At 19h30, it is noted that due to some misunderstanding, an order to retire caused evacuation of front trenches. Captain J. MacDonald rallied the troops as they fell back into Parsons Road, but advancing with his permanent garrison of B Company, he reoccupied the abandoned trenches with little opposition. The troops who had retired then re-advanced and the situation was saved. The withdrawal spread to the rear of the brigade and almost became a panic. Fugitives began streaming down Oxford Street past the HQ and there was some difficulty in stopping the rush and getting them to return to their units. For two days after the battle, all units were kept busy gathering up arms, equipment and ammunition that were disseminated on the field, as well as holding the captured positions.

On the afternoon of July 15, "C" and "D" Companies took over trenches on the west of Achi Baba nullah from the Plymouth Battalion while "A" Company relieved part of the Drake Battalion and the 6th HLI Battalion. During the night, members of this latter Company crept furtively to the Horse Shoe Trench to re-install signalling equipment in a proper state for ensuring communications. On July 16, "C" Company recovered fifteen asphyxiating bombs from a penthouse in one of the nullah trenches thanks to the information given by a captured Turkish officer who disapproved of such a German innovation. The next 48 hours were employed by fortifying defences, completing the wiring for communications and the burial of over forty Turks between trenches F11 and F12, the former trench densely packed with corpses had to be filled in.

On July 18, "A", "C" and "D" Companies were relieved by the 6th East Lancashire Battalion and had to trudge less than three miles, taking four full hours to reach a place of rest where hot stew, potatoes and lots if tea were provided before laying down on blankets to sleep. "B" Company arrived the next morning after moving during the dark hours. The battalion stayed in the Rest Camp for twenty-one days. Anyone who associates the name of this site with the notion of a Holiday Camp has been grossly misled! These were not really camps at all and were sometimes referred to as Rest Trenches, but in the military sense, they were not even regarded as trenches and were far from being restful.

The area was a bare expanse of clay soil trodden hard, powdered with heavy dust turned into sticky mud at the slightest bit of rain. It was bounded on the north side by a ragged hedge which sheltered the remnants left by the previous tenants' bad housekeeping in the form of discarded clothing, empty meat and jam cans and other rubbish. On the south side, the ground fell into a gradual slope for 200 metres culminating in the dry bed of a ditch or streamlet beyond which a row of trees concealed the partial dugouts of the Divisional Staff as their permanent quarters. After levelling out and then rising again to form a ridge, the ground dropped down to the sea. The parapets were ragged, irregular and rarely bulletproof. There were few sandbags (priority given to the front lines) and no form of overhead cover. Shade from the sun was obtained by stretching ground sheets or blankets overhead.

In the intense heat, with the exposure of battle wounds, the invasion of flies at all times and especially when men were eating food, the lack of proper hygiene and a monotonous diet of canned food (bully beef), all in difficult living conditions, many men suffered and died from the spread of dysentery and disease. After the authorities recognised this, they made fresh meat (frozen) available, as well as desiccated vegetables and rice, and bread in the place of hard biscuits. Rest time of two hours between 2 pm and 4 pm was instituted thus suspending non-urgent fatigues. However, the overall strength of the troops was depleted by 5 to 10 per cent per month due to hospitalisation of those very sick. During all this time, the area, despite not being in the front line, was subjected to shelling and gunfire

It was the habit, when taking munitions to the front line, to bring back wounded men. On one occasion, when returning from this task, Nick bent over a groaning wounded Turkish soldier to see what aid he could give him, when the soldier suddenly swung up his bayoneted rifle which fortunately slipped between his armpits. This provoked an automatic reaction that led him to kick the man in his head and kill him, leaving himself with a sore foot for several days. It is an event that obviously marked Nick's mind, judging from the fact that he recounted this to me, not very often, but more than once. That's war; suddenly, there is an unexpected aggression provoking swift reaction, a fatal issue, then the outcome leaves an unforgettable scar in one's memory box.

Between July 19 and 22, the battalion was put on fatigues, partly at the disposal of the 29th Division and also working to link up the Rest Trenches in order to speed up inter-communications. Officers and men slept in boots with equipment and ammunition beside them ready for rapid moves. Before leaving the Rest Camp, all ranks were inoculated against cholera. On August 6, the 29th and 42nd Divisions attacked the Turks, gaining some ground, as a diversion during the first landings to take place at Suvla Bay, 15 miles up the Aegean coast, at the same time as advances were made by the troops from Anzac Cove. While the Turks stemmed the attack at Suvla Bay, the diversionary attack cost terrible losses as most of the gains made at Cap Helles were annulled by August 7 except for the forward position of the "Vineyard" (between Krithia and Achi Baba nullahs) held by the 42nd Division.

By 11 p.m., "A" and "B" Companies were installed in the Eski line to the east of the nullah, with the Battalion HQ on the inner flank, while "C" and "D" Companies with the Machine Gun Section occupied the line west of the small nullah. The whole position though more than 1000 yards from the firing line was not particularly safe from such desultory fire going on in front. On August 12, determined Turkish attacks enabled them to regain the "Vineyard" position but the remaining British positions held out. From then on until the end of October, life tended to become monotonous with the Turks clearly not intending to attack. The allies continued to further the network of trenches with the aim of approaching the Turkish lines for mining operations, thus keeping the men busy on fatigues. At the same time, disease and dysentery continued to take its toll.

Nick also contracted dysentery but survived and returned to Scotland on October 28, 1915. He was then destined to spend a year convalescing in different hospitals in Edinburgh. Little did he know then that one day in the future he would put foot again on Turkish soil. As for those who stayed behind and escaped death, their campaign ended in January 1916 when the operation was recognised to be a failure and the Expeditionary Force was evacuated from Gallipoli.

Nick had a very low opinion of the British generals, for their dourness, insensitivity and particularly the way the war had been conducted in that campaign[11]. Many a time, men were sent "over the top" when it was clear that they had no chance of advancing without being slaughtered. He was full of admiration for the courage and fighting valour of the Anzacs (Australian and New Zealand Army Corps). He also had great respect for the Turks whom he considered to be fine soldiers; they were reputed to be extremely correct and humane in their treatment of the prisoners who fell into their hands. It has been recorded that at times, a truce was agreed upon for the sole purpose of allowing each side to proceed with the burial of their dead. The belligerents talked together and mingled without animosity, but with respect and cordiality, and even with regret at the end of the truce for having to return to the awful task of waging war[12].

Convalescence in Scotland 1915–1916

Apart from the fact that Nick had dysentery, there are no records available to indicate for what ills or injuries he was treated in different hospitals at the end of 1915 and during 1916. It was in this particular period that, like many soldiers at that time, he kept an album of photos as well as of friendly drawings and poems dedicated by his comrades and attendant nurses. It is interesting to peruse these archives that picture some of the thoughts and realities of this period, (so they appear in an annexe at the end of this book).

When looking back at the photo taken just after enlistment (September 25, 1914), we can see that the soldiers now convalescing who survived the initial combats of the war, have matured and are men who have faced injuries and death at the battlefront, and forever carry the memory of lost comrades. Gone is the carefree look of youth.

It can be seen from the chronology of the photos taken during this convalescence that he frequently moved between three hospitals, most likely for special examinations at different sites. From the dates shown on these documents, there is an indication of where Nick was cared for in the vicinity of Edinburgh, notably:

(i) Edinburgh War Hospital, Bangour (outside of Edinburgh in the west); it was originally an asylum situated in very large grounds. It was requisitioned by the War Office in the 1914–1918 War for the wounded

---

[11] See Lt Col David Murray a Contributed Paper: 52nd Lowland Division at Gallipoli – a Second Flodden, in Annex

[12] Kevin Fewster, Vecihi and Hatice Hürmüz Başarın, Gallipoli, The Turkish Story, Allen and Unwin, Crow's nest, NSW, Australia

troops and served again in the Second World War. When I visited it in July 2007, the area was totally abandoned but it was on the threshold of becoming a high-class real estate development project but not yet fully determined. I took a bus from Edinburgh to visit this area and I recognised some of the buildings from the photos in Nick's album of souvenirs. It was quite a moving moment to think that I was treading the earth where Nick had spent months recovering from his first war wounds. He left many photos taken in this area.

(ii) Mayfield Hospital was in the heart of Edinburgh city, formerly a Blind People's Institute.

(iii) The Royal Victoria Hospital also in Edinburgh, at 13 Craigleith Road, near the Western General Hospital, has transferred many of its functions to other hospitals but still operates services for the elderly.

At Royal Victoria Hospital June 20, 1916 – My father, hands in pockets, is standing on group's right-hand side

Fighting in the Somme as from 1917

From the autumn of 1916 to the end of that year, no more notes nor photographic records are to be found in Nick's archives and this is probably explained that during this time, he must have undergone a new period of military training because on January 2, 1917, he was incorporated in the British Expeditionary Force to France to fight in the Somme. As his original battalion, 1/5th H.L.I., after the abandonment of the Dardanelles in 1916, had gone on to fight in other areas of the Middle East, he was thus transferred in January 1917 to the 17th battalion H.L.I. engaged on the Somme war front[13]. The 17th Bn H.L.I. was part of the 97th brigade within the 32nd Division, 5th (V) Army of the British Expeditionary Force France.

It must be remembered that from the Channel coast right down to the Swiss border, it was a continuous line of trenches necessitating the mobilisation of huge numbers of men and material for front line action, plus as many men for ensuring relief of those in the front line at regular intervals, as well as the logistics for maintaining continuous supplies of food and ammunition, medical care, the disposal of the dead, staff and commanding organisations, etc. The disposition of all the different allied units, French, British, Australian, New Zealand, Indian, Belgian, Portuguese and others required the delimitation of areas of responsibility and close coordination put in place by the political powers.

The background to this theatre of war that Nick was entering at the outset of 1917, consisted of the important gains made by the Allies during 1916, especially in the latter part of that year. As a result of these advances, the Germans commenced a strategic retreat to lay behind lines chosen to give them greater defence security. Naturally, the allies intended no respite for the enemy and acted to benefit from the impetus of their advance and to consolidate their gains. The weather conditions were appalling as the winter of 1916/1917 was the coldest one of all the war.

After Nick's first war experience taking place in the terrible heat of the summer of 1915 in Turkey, he had now to face the bleak, winter climate in the Somme, operating in mud and knee deep in water-filled trenches, with freezing temperatures. On top of the exposure to enemy

---

[13] This re-assignment was found with the aid of the National Archives at Kew through the coding of the medal awards. So far, the exact company in this new battalion to which he was drafted has not been determined, but with this basic information, it has been made possible to obtain copies of the War Diaries relating the movements and events of the 17th Battalion HLI during the two and a half months fighting in the Somme until March 12, 1917 at which point my father was shipped back to England for medical care.

shelling, gunfire and gas bombs, he told me that he suffered from frostbite, shrapnel wounds and the effects of those gas bomb attacks. He did say that in certain moments of military inactivity, there had been times of fraternisation with the German troops, and in conversation, he mentioned that there was compassion for the ordinary enemy soldier who was subjected to the same risks and fate of war as his own companions. Nick also mentioned to me that while in the lines, an officer would at times come up to a man on guard, drowsing because tired of staying so long in water-filled trenches, and the officer would take away his rifle, then ask the guard where it was – the man was then shot at dawn! He also talked of the high regard he had for the French soldiers fighting nearby in the Somme.

These remarks on the conditions of life in the trenches that I recall from Nick's talks were certainly not exaggerated when perusing the information recorded in the 17th H.L.I.'s War Diaries and the various writings on this period, for a good part based on the War Diaries. However, no mention is made in the diaries I read about fraternisation or on the shooting of soldiers considered to be deficient in their duties, but these events did take place.

**An extract from the 17ᵗʰ battalion of the H.L.I.'s Record of War Service
1914–1918 sums up the events of the New Year 1917:
The Somme
The Seventeenth Highland Light Infantry
(Glasgow Chamber of Commerce Battalion)
Record of War Service, 1914–1918**

Extract – The New Year, 1917

*Bad weather – Courcelles – trench labours – varied moves – beginning of
Spring Offensive – attack by the French – the advance – Nesle – condition of
inhabitants – great digging work at Germaine.*

*The opening months of the New Year were months of battling not only
against a human enemy, but also against the elements and the bad conditions
that they created. The winter of 1916 had been a severe one, and in passing into
1917, it continued its course with unabated severity. The battalion left Rubempré
on January 6 and partly by motor lorry and partly in column of route proceeded
to Courcelles where, on the following day, they relieved the troops of the 3ʳᵈ
Division in the trenches opposite Serre. The weather was bad, the enemy kept up
brisk attentions and the trenches were the worst that the battalion had ever been
in. Most of them were absolutely impassable, being full of water to a height of
five feet, with the result that relief had for the most part to be made outside the
trenches. Owing to these material conditions, strict orders were issued for the
prevention of "trench feet", but notwithstanding every precaution, several cases
occurred.*

*Heavy and continuous work was put in mending and bettering the trenches,
training the drafts that were arriving, performing tactical exercises and battalion
routine affairs. By this time, several ceremonies had taken place at which
decorations were bestowed upon NCOs and men for bravery in the Field and
gallantry in action. Esprit de corps was stronger than ever, while the
establishment of special strong posts relieved the tediousness of trench labours,
also by minor raids on the Bosche, and when out of the line by football and such
recreations as the circumstances permitted. This type of campaigning was
experienced during January and February at Courcelles, Beaumont Hamel,
Lyntham Camp, Mailly-Maillet, Bolton Camp, Molliens-au-Bois (where on
February 19, 1917, Major F.R.F. Sworder, Gordon Highlanders, assumed
temporary command as Colonel Paul, after being hospitalised in France, was sent
to England where he was appointed to a home unit), Then it was Camon,
Wiencourt, Le Quesnel. In March, the approach of spring seemed to bring with*

it nothing but additional storms of rain and snow, and the names of such points in the line as Key Post and Kuropatkin will bring back memories of buttressing up collapsed trenches and mending wire entanglements. The French attacked on March 16 etc.

The War Diary – La Somme 1917

While the summary above resumes well the soldiers' overall conditions at the front during this period, in reciting the details of the War Diaries covering the 24 hours day by day, event by event, the extensive and unceasing demands on the men's energy and courage in the face of danger, is revealed below much more vividly[14].

Although Nick was assigned to The British Expeditionary Force France as from January 2, 1917, this date is most likely the date when he actually left Scotland and not the date at which he arrived at the front. However, it is interesting to see the account of the actions of the 17th battalion day by day as from the first of January 1917 at Rubempré in the Somme as recorded in the War Diaries.

Official summaries of this campaign have been made, as shown in the extract above, but the interest of including the detailed day-by-day reports recorded in the War Diary stresses the real conditions of daily life on the front such as: delays in being relieved, the prolonged adverse weather conditions, the length of time remaining in waterlogged trenches, continued activity behind the lines limiting periods of rest before returning to the front line, such as fatigues for rebuilding trenches damaged by rain, repairing barbed wire installations, patrols at night, exercises, etc. This daily detail may seem lengthy reading, but it gives a better understanding of the ordeal's reality of these dedicated men and it is almost a respectful accompaniment and salute to their courage.

The War Diary reports as follows:

Rubempré, January 1, 1917, tactical exercise carried out in conjunction with the 16th battalion H.L.I. In the afternoon, the Battalion Team won the Divisional Football Championship by beating the 2nd Battalion Inniskillins Fusiliers in the final by 7 goals to 3. The bayonet fighting team took part in the Brigade Competition. Col Paul received command of the battalion on his return from leave. The battalion is ordered to hold itself in readiness to move up to the line. January 2, parades today under company arrangements: bombing, bayonet fighting, and c. Commanding Officer and Company Commanders visited trenches today. On January 3, battalion supplied large fatigue parties today for

---

[14] In annex are shown an example of a page of the War Diary (Crown Copyright) now located at The National Archives at Kew as well as the transcription I made of these journals into six pages in order to provide a more readable document.

work at Puchevillers. The remainder of battalion paraded under Company arrangements. January 4, battalion paraded at 7.10 a.m. and proceeded beyond Puchevillers where tactical exercises were carried out in conjunction with 16ᵗʰ battalion H.L.I. Weather extremely wet. Afternoon parades cancelled. Foot inspections took place in billets. Working parties supplied for work on ranges. January 5 – Bathing at Puchevillers – parades by Companies as per Bat. Orders of 4ᵗʰ inst. See 4. January 6 – left Rubempré 7.30 a.m. by motor lorries to Bus-en-Artois and thereafter in columns of route to Courcelles where we took over billets – arrived at 11.30 a.m. Military Crosses were awarded to 2 Captains and a Company-Sergeant-Major, and a Distinguished Conduct Medal to a Sergeant.

Trenches – January 7, battalion into trenches – sub-sector C.3 relieving 3ʳᵈ Division troops at 5 p.m., relief completed at 8.10 p.m. – night quiet except for intermittent shelling. A. B. and C. Companies in line – D Company in support. January 8 – Patrol left our line at 11.30 p.m. (7 Jan 1917) to examine wire in front of outpost between Blénau and southern Trench; parts require strengthening. Patrol returned 12.30 a.m. Enemy shelled Rob Roy and Monk Trenches between 6.45 a.m. and 7.15 a.m., enemy Trench Mortars (T.M.s) active against Rob Roy. Heavy rain during night, trenches in a bad state. Pumping being carried out – our artillery very active in afternoon against enemy trenches – enemy's reply weak. January 9 Weather still bad. Pumping going on – patrol-examined wire between N° 3 and N°4 Posts – found a good obstacle. Artillery bombardment of enemy lines opposite battalion frontage started at 8 a.m. today and has continued throughout the day with varying intensity. Good shooting was observed. Enemy replied weakly against Rob Roy and Monk Trenches.

Courcelles – January 10 – Bad weather continues – pumping going on – the night was quiet on our frontage. Artillery again subjected the enemy trenches to a severe bombardment that continued throughout the whole day. The TMs cooperated in the afternoon. The enemy's retaliation was more brisk than usual, being especially heavy at the time of the relief that was delayed. On relief, the battalion proceeded to Courcelles and took over billets. Casualties during the spell were five Other Ranks (OR) wounded. Seven Officers joined the battalion yesterday. January 11 – cleaning up, foot inspection etc. Large carrying parties go for rations and water being supplied tonight. Draft of 11 OR joined the battalion.

Trenches – January 12 – prepare for going into line – gumboots issued to all ranks – each carry three pairs of socks – rubbing feet with whale oil. Trenches of sub-section C3 taken over from 11ᵗʰ Border Regt. – relief completed 12.50 a.m. January 13 – night relatively quiet – 4a.m. enemy barrage with 77mm shells on Rob Roy and Monk Trenches – support trench shelled with 5.9s. Artillery retaliation given – forenoon enemy artillery active South Matthew Copse and in K.29 C. Situation normal in the afternoon – our artillery slightly active in the evening. Sleet all day – conditions bad – pumping trenches continued. January 14 – night calm. About 5 a.m. enemy was shelling our trenches with more than *average intermittency. Our artillery was asked to retaliate – intense fire on enemy trenches for five minutes. At 5.30 and 5.50 a.m., enemy shelling ceased – very misty – visibility of enemy trenches difficult. Relief by 16th Lancashire Fusiliers commenced at 6 p.m. – late in evening, Colincamp Rd and artillery emplacements shelled with tear shells.*

Bus-en-Artois – January 15 – relief completed early morning – day spent resting – cleaning up – foot inspection and rifle inspection. Small fatigue parties supplied. January 16 – Large fatigue parties supplied by battalion for work on roads etc. bad weather – heavy snowfall. Draft of seven Other Ranks joined battalion. January 17 – Large fatigue parties supplied by battalion – weather still bad – snow continues – rifle inspection etc. January 18 – Large fatigue parties supplied by battalion – battalion concert tonight. January 19 – large fatigue parties supplied by battalion – Rifle inspection.

Trenches – January 20 – 17th battalion H.L.I. relieved 9th Devons in brigade reserve in Beaumont-Hamel. Two Companies in Q M a. 8.8 – two Companies in the Burn Work. Relief took place in afternoon – beginning of hard frost. January 21 – Hard frost and sunshine – battalion supplied fatigues to Royal Engineers 8 Officers and 195 Other Ranks. January 22 – Severe frost and sunshine – low visibility – Company Commander meeting at 10.30 a.m. – fatigues supplied for carrying salvage and gumboots. January 23 – A and D Companies and half battalion HQ relieved 11th Border Regt. In R1 sub-sector. Half battalion HQ was at Station Road. B and C Companies stayed in Q M a. 8.8 in support and furnished fatigue parties as follows – 3 Officers and 150 Other Ranks for Auchonvilliers and 2 Officers and 50 Other Ranks for Mailly Maillet. Victory Post established. January 24 – Polls Perch established – Lines were taped to stress posts – Patrols were out in R.1.a and encountered hostile patrols who were challenged and answered 11.3 11th Company 3rd Bavarian R.I.R. January 25 – B and C Companies relieved A and D Companies in R1 sub-sector. Patrols encountered a hostile patrol on ridge in R.1.a. January 26 – A battle patrol left Victory post o attack hostile post situation R.1.a. Artillery barrage for 10 minutes during which patrol crept into position – the post was carried but no enemy in garrison – signs of enemy tracks in vicinity. Two courts of enquiry held.

Beaumont-Hamel Dugouts – January 27 – B and C Companies 17th H.L.I. were relieved by two Companies of 16th H.L.I. – the whole battalion withdrew to dugouts in Beaumont Hamel in Brigade Reserve. Working parties of 200 yards were formed each night to work in artillery lines. Three men wounded in Royal Engineer fatigues. January 28 – A defence of Beaumont-Hamel drawn up as follows: Stuarts, Campbells, Harpers, Hamilton and Burn Work. Fatigues were formed during night as usual.

Trenches – January 29 – The battalion relieved 11th Border Regt. In R 2 sub-sector – A and D Companies in front line – B and C Companies in support. Patrols report: enemy posts near Waggon Road close to Tentree Alley. January

30 – Artillery carried out stunts on K36 d at 7.45 and 8.45 p.m. – also on R.1. at midnight – various parties of enemy seen during the day. January 31 – at 5 p.m., enemy carried out a Hurricane bombardment with trench mortars on our left Company front – first appearances of mortars – artillery carried out observed fire on same during the day.

Lytham Camp – February 1 – On morning of February 1, battalion was relieved in R. 2. Sub-sector and marched to Lytham Camp. Day spent cleaning up generally – Companies paraded for rifle inspection. February 2 – Supplied a working party of one Officer and 20 Other Ranks to 219ᵗʰ Field Company Royal Engineers – haversack rations carried – bathing done during the day.

Lytham Camp – February 1 – On morning of February 1, battalion was relieved in R. 2. Sub-sector and marched to Lytham Camp. Day spent cleaning up generally – Companies paraded for rifle inspection. February 2 – Supplied a working party of one Officer and 20 Other Ranks to 219ᵗʰ Field Company Royal Engineers – haversack rations carried – bathing done during the day.

Beaumont-Hamel Dugouts – January 27 – B and C Companies 17ᵗʰ H.L.I. were relieved by two Companies of 16ᵗʰ H.L.I. – the whole battalion withdrew to dugouts in Beaumont Hamel in Brigade Reserve. Working parties of 200 yards were formed each night to work in artillery lines. Three men wounded in Royal Engineer fatigues. January 28 – A defence of Beaumont-Hamel drawn up as follows: Stuarts, Campbells, Harpers, Hamilton and Burn Work. Fatigues were formed during night as usual.

Trenches – January 29 – The battalion relieved 11ᵗʰ Border Regt. In R 2 sub-sector – A and D Companies in front line – B and C Companies in support. Patrols report: enemy posts near Waggon Road close to Tentree Alley. January 30 – Artillery carried out stunts on K36 d at 7.45 and 8.45 p.m. – also on R.1. at midnight – various parties of enemy seen during the day. January 31 – at 5 p.m., enemy carried out a Hurricane bombardment with trench mortars on our left Company front – first appearances of mortars – artillery carried out observed fire on same during the day.

Lytham Camp – February 1 – On morning of February 1, battalion was relieved in R. 2. Sub-sector and marched to Lytham Camp. Day spent cleaning up generally – Companies paraded for rifle inspection. February 2 – Supplied a working party of one Officer and 20 Other Ranks to 219ᵗʰ Field Company Royal Engineers – haversack rations carried – bathing done during the day.

Trenches – February 3 – Night of 2/3ʳᵈ battalion relieved 11ᵗʰ Border Regt. In R 1 sub-sector – Colonel W. J. Paul admitted to F. A. Major J. K. Muir took over command of the battalion. Two Patrols sent, each one Officer one Sergeant + five Other Ranks to locate and report on enemy positions. First Patrol left Polls Perch on a bearing of 29° magnetic of 100 yards, then east 400 yards on a bearing of 92° mag. – Patrol proceeded to east of Glory lane. Second Patrol left FIG Post on a bearing of 8° mag. For 300 yards to reconnoitre the enemy's position. Two Other Ranks to Cadet School England. February 4 – In early morning our B

Company made a faint attack on Point 55 in cooperation with Royal Naval Division who were carrying out an attack on our right – B Company after going 50 yards beyond Gun Post met with heavy machine gun fire from both left and right flanks, also assisted by enemy barrage of shrapnel – owing to clear visibility of night it was deemed not advisable to continue any further and the command withdrew to our original front line trench given by officer in charge of the operation – carried out in good order, only two casualties reported both from machine gun fire – in evening front line, sand posts subjected to heavy artillery barrage. February 5 – morning about 2 a.m. till 4 a.m., our front line and posts heavily shelled – the enemy also sent over a lot of tear shells bursting all around our posts – on account of an expected counter-attack, companies stood to in their various posts – in the evening we were relieved in R. 1. Sub-sector by 16th Lancashire Fusiliers – relief completed by midnight.

Beaumont-Hamel Dugouts – February 6 – after being relieved, we withdrew to dugouts in Beaumont-Hamel and relieved the 2nd Kings Own Yorkshire Light Infantry – completed by 1 a.m. – the battalion supplied carrying parties. A draft of 42 Other Ranks arrived for duty within the battalion – 9 Other Ranks to Cadet School in England. February 7 – The battalion supplied carrying parties and also working parties. Night of 7th/8th, we relieved 16th HLI in R.2 sub-sector – our C Company taking over the Posts.

Trenches – February 8 – Companies supplied carrying parties, strengthened Posts, dug latrines and cleared part of front-line trenches – night of 8th/9th, D Company relieved C Company on the Posts. February 9 – Patrols sent out to reconnoitre and locate exact dispositions of enemy – we also strengthened our posts having been blown in – our B Company relieved D Company on the Posts on night of 9th and 10th. February 10 – night of 10th/11th A Company relieved D Company on Posts – B Company withdrew and stood to in close support to King's Own Yorkshire Light Infantry under orders to move at any moment if such support required. Casualties as follows: 2nd Lt A. R. Moon wounded, one Other Rank died of wounds and eight Other Ranks wounded. We furnish escorts for prisoners. 2nd Lt C. S. Williamson arrived as reinforcement. February 11 – Companies supplied carrying parties and clearing trenches that had been blown in – we furnish escorts for prisoners. February 12 – the battalion relieved the 2nd King's Own Yorkshire Light Infantry in Tentree and Lager alleys in the morning – our casualties: Capt. A.G. Marshall, 2nd Lt R.W. Smith killed, also one Other Rank killed and eight Other Ranks wounded – we sent out a patrol to locate the exact position of a German post which we intended attacking in the morning. 2nd Lt W. G. King and 2nd Lt G. W. M. Patterson as reinforcements. Four Other Ranks to Cadet School England.

Mailly Mallet – February 13 – at 7.30 a.m., C Company attacked an enemy post but before reaching the post they were met by enemy in superior numbers – C Company were forced to fall back – the Germans managed to occupy our post but we reinforced C Company with part of A Company and two Platoons of

King's Own Yorkshire Light Infantry and we successfully counter attacked and drove back the enemy to his original position. The same night, we were relieved in Tentree and Lager Alleys by 2ⁿᵈ King's Own Yorkshire Light Infantry – on being relieved battalion withdrew to billets in Mailly Mallet leaving A Company in support of 2ⁿᵈ KOYLI. Casualties: four Other Ranks killed, 15 Other Ranks wounded, 2ⁿᵈ Lt Bullar wounded, 18 missing, nine missing believed prisoners.

Bolton Camp – February 14 – about 4 p.m., the battalion left Mailly Mallet and marched to huts at Bolton Camp. Capt. A. J. Scully of 2ⁿᵈ Manchester Regiment assumed temporary command of battalion – spent day cleaning up, etc. February 15 – companies continued cleaning up – inspections held under company arrangements – 2ⁿᵈ Lt S. L. Brodie in reinforcement. February 16 – battalion inspected in full marching order by Commanding Officer – bathing carried out during the day.

Molliens-au-Bois – February 17 – The battalion moved from Bolton Camp to billets in Molliens-au-Bois on buses – 2 Other Ranks to Cadet School England. February 18 – the battalion on Church parade at 10.30 a.m. – companies completed cleaning up – billet areas were cleaned up and rubbish disposed of. Two Other Ranks to Cadet School England. February 19 – Companies paraded for physical drill, close order drill and manual exercises. Battalion paraded at 11.30 a.m. and Capt. A.J. Scully M.C. handed over same to Major F.R.F. Sworder who assumed temporary command from this date. Capt. A.J. Scully M.C. was struck off the strength of battalion. Draft of 12 Other Ranks arrived for duty with battalion – Capt. Mayer Renfrogment. February 20 – inspection of billets and physical training – bombing carried out under instructors – companies paraded for musketry, squad drill, bayonet fighting and close order drill – a football match was arranged with 219ᵗʰ Field Company Royal Engineers, but owing to weather condition it was postponed – a draft of 9 Other Ranks arrived for duty with the battalion.

Camon – February 21 – the battalion marched from Molliens-au-Bois to billets in Camon.

Wiencourt – February 22 – The battalion marched from Camon to billets in Wiencourt. February 23 – Companies paraded for inspection and cleaned up generally – fatigue parties detailed: one N C O. and 6 men to report for work with Town Mayor – draft of 31 Other Ranks arrived for duty with battalion. – February 24 – Companies paraded for bombing, bayonet fighting and close order drill – one of the last drafts was inspected by the Commanding Officer – one Other Rank was sent to Cadet School England.

Le Quesnel – February 25 – the battalion marched from Wiencourt to billets in Le Quesnel – one Other Tanks sent to Cadet School England – February 26 – parades under Company arrangements cleaning up etc. – February 27 – Companies paraded for billet inspection, physical training, bombing, bayonet fighting and close order drill – Commanding Officer parade (I) Promulgation of Courts Martial as ordered today (II) battalion drill. February 28 – The battalion paraded in full marching order as strong as possible for inspection by General Officer Commanding 32nd Division following which Companies did physical training, bombing, bayonet fighting and close order drill – drafts of 57 Other Ranks arrived for duty with the battalion – one Other Ranks sent to Cadet School England. March 1 – Reveille 7 a.m. breakfast 8 a.m. – during day routine as designated in programme of work carried through under Company arrangement.

Trenches – March 2 – Reveille 7 a.m. breakfast 8 a.m. blankets stored preparatory to battalion moving into line. At 8.30 p.m., battalion left its quarters and proceeded to Beaufort where packs were stored – later, it moves into the trenches end of Rouvroy and Battalion HQ were established at Ney Post – the conditions on taking over from 16th Newfoundland Regt. Were active: a heavy enemy shell fire aiming on the front and communication trenches – unfortunately, 1 L/Cpl and 6 men were wounded as casualties on entry, the first being killed and others wounded by grenade fire – the stores and transport took up quarters at Beaufort. March 3 – battalion was holding right sub-sector of brigade line with 16th HLI on the left, XI Border Regt. In support at Kuropatkin, and 2nd King's Own Yorkshire Light Infantry in reserve at Warvillers. All Companies held the front line, activity on both sides was moderate in the hostile sense and our artillery seemed to be registering on various targets during the day with several bursts of rapid fire in the evening – enemy fire a few shells into Rouvroy and surrounding wads, but was more active with grenades and spring bombs some of which were of the gas type – good useful work done in clearing trenches parts in bad condition owing to mud and want of repair – weather : dry and dull; wind, gentle S.E. March 4 – work of cleaning and repairing trenches continued and in several parts mud has been entirely cleared and communication greatly facilitated – digging of new latrines started – work of intelligence was carried through and much valuable trench information obtained and noted – artillery on both sides much more active and aerial observation much more in evidence – two patrols left our lines during the night to reconnoitre no man's land on the immediate front – weather: bright sunshine during the day with heavy snowfall lasting fully six hours during the night.

Kuropatkin – March 5 – work of cleaning and repairing trenches and making new latrines was continued but with much slower progress owing to melting snow – artillery decidedly of greater activity on both sides, while trench mortars used by enemy against our front line: many of latter missiles contained gas – aerial darts were used against our support line – in the evening, battalion was relieved by XI Borders and took up position of brigade support in trenches – relief was completed by 11 p.m. without incident –battalion HQ, A and C Companies established quarters at Kuropatkin – B Company in dugouts at Rouvroy and D Company at St Nicolas Post in the rear of left battalion. March 6 – battalion supplies two companies for trench cleaning under Royal Engineers while others cleaned rifles and equipment – at this new post, little or no enemy shelling was directed though there is evidence that at some previous date the immediate vicinity had received the attention of enemy artillery – this was a fairly quiet day for both sides of artillery; that of the enemy being principally directed to roads and battery emplacements in Rouvroy 50 "heavies" (a large proportion being tear gas shells) fell. Weather, bright sunshine – our airplanes carried out observation during the morning and some heavy black shrapnel was directed against them with a wonderful misjudgement of range. March 7 – during the day, every available man worked at an allocated task of cleaning trenches; some Companies in brigade orders and the others to those issued by battalion. This day, a shelling report form was issued to the gas guard and the result proved a fair success – again in early morning, our airplanes were active and two machines patrolled the line – enemy artillery, light and heavy, were decidedly attentive to Rouvroy and a fair proportion of the shells were lachrymatory – weather: bright at first, dulling later with slight snow fall and keen frost at night.

Ney Post – March 8 – battalion supplied two companies for trench clearing, while two other companies engaged carrying bombs preparatory to moving into line – at 5 p.m. relief of XI borders started and at 10.15 p.m., was completed without incident – during this night remarkable quietude reigned over the trenches and even the shelling of the rear was less than usual – two patrols left our lines and carried out a fairly good examination of enemy wire – weather: bright, clear and frosty with a gentle breeze freshening towards night. March 9 – during day, battalion continued cleaning trenches and repairing posts – at night all companies wired gap and front line – a small patrol left D Company and examined the jumping off trench on their front – enemy activity much more in evidence than usual and heavy Trench Mortars, rifle grenades and gas shells fell with irritating regularity on our front line, though of long duration this bombardment was not intense and the damage was less than expected – our wiring suffered at secured posts and some casualties occurred: wounded six Other Ranks; gassed (slightly) two Other Ranks; S.I.W. (Self Inflicted Wounds): 1 Other Ranks – shelling of the rear heavy at times and much gas thrown into Rouvroy. Lt Col Sworder joined the Bn from conference of senior officers and Capt. Muir left to join 15th HLI – weather fresh with gentle N.E. Wind. March 10 – the freshening after frost worked badly on trenches and much labour was necessary to keep the trenches clear – all companies engaged on this task during the day – wiring strengthened by all companies – enemy shelling continued as briskly as previous day and Rouvroy Road suffered much from gas shells – a considerable number of Trench Mortars were thrown into our lines but the casualties were not heavy, only two men being wounded – gas shells fell into our lines though not in sufficient numbers to become more that local danger – one Machine Gun was damaged and put out of action, but another was immediately drawn from reserve in its place – weather: dull and moist – damp mist rendering observation difficult – wind S.E. gentle. March 11 – overnight further freshening of atmospheric conditions worked havoc on trenches and in many parts trenches fell in. Every available man set to work clearing obstructions and much *improvement attained. Enemy artillery quieter than usual, though about 6 p.m. a very heavy bombardment was observed some distance on the right, our machines carried out aeroplane observation in the morning and about 11 a.m. a German bi-plane was driven off by our artillery. Our 4.2" and 6"howitzers played havoc on the enemy front line and silenced the German Trench Mortar which has so actively bombarded our lines during the past two days. One self-inflicted wounded was reported during the day. A patrol left our lines about midnight and discovered an enemy working party repairing their wire and returned 2 hours later without accident. Weather fine, gentle S.E. wind freshening later and bringing heavy rain.*

The End Of Nick's Service In The Somme

These daily reports, from a military and procedural standpoint, reflect the official routine of witnessing not only events but also the accomplishment of orders and the application of the strategy imposed. Of course, no mention is made here of the relationship between the men, their solidarity, their sense of humour despite dire circumstances, their suffering and the instability of their morale. It's not surprising that at some point there was a tendency to mutiny.

We can see how long the battalion often remained in trenches before being relieved, this duration varying according to circumstances from 2 to 5 days. After relief, if they were lucky and not retired to simple "dug-outs" they could sleep in temporary billets, except for those periods when night work was ordered such as patrols, mending barbed wire fences near the lines, transporting rations, ammunition and material. Inspections of feet and of arms cleaned automatically took place after returning from front line trenches. It should be recalled that at this time the allies were progressing forward as the German army was retreating eastwards to a strengthened line of defence.

Nick, now on the official list of the wounded, left this war zone on March 12 for hospitalisation in the Queen Mary's Military Hospital at Whalley in Lancashire. According to Nick's army records, his posting to the British Expeditionary Force France terminated on March 12, 1917 on arrival in Britain on the 13th and therefore as far as his presence on the war front was concerned, he must have already been on his way to embark on a ship heading for Southampton after March 10.

Convalescence In Lancashire - Demobilisation

So far, we have no records of his itinerary after the end of Nick's service on March 12 but judging from three poems dedicated to him, presumably by nurses who indicated Queen Mary's military Hospital in Whalley in Lancashire, with their signature between April and

September 1917, it is there that he was in convalescence. When I visited this hospital at Whalley, the Director kindly took me around and then let me take pictures of old photos that show during the Great War, that the railway line was extended to bring the war casualties directly into the hospital grounds after their having boarded the train at Southampton at disembarkation. This is just another indication of the immense number of war victims necessitating the installation of new amenities and the adaptation of existing ones to accommodate the huge regular influx of the wounded.

Despite research at the Kew National Archives and at the Lancashire Records Office in Preston, no medical records for him are available, many archives having been destroyed by enemy attacks during the 2nd World War, but details of the medals awarded him were available. The only subsequent written records are the papers of his discharge with effect at April 6, 1918 and his final pay slip, which are part of his existing personal records. On this latter document, his home address is stated as 11 Airlie Gardens, (in fact Airlie Street) Hyndland (Partick), Glasgow[15]. Among other things on these records, his trade on enlistment is marked "Engineer", "Total Service with the Colours: 3 years 7 months and 25 days", and there is a physical description which states: "Height 5' 6"", "No Identification Marks, Complexion: Sallow, Eyes: Grey and Hair: Dark-brown".

In the course of the occasional talks about the First World War with me, I felt that there was never any hate of the enemy as such in the front line. His disgust and criticism were directed against those in power on either side politically and militarily. Looking back at his wartime experience, the tragic loss of his companions in the front line or through military discipline he could never forget.

---

[15] In fact, the address is officially 11 Airlie Street, but generally called Gardens at the time because the architect had the name Airlie Gardens largely sculptured in the stone of the building at the far end of the street. This led to great difficulty when trying to locate the site, which I did, enabling me to take photos of my father's former home until 1920 when he left to work in France (this address is confirmed in the 1920 Electoral list which also included his brother Joseph who had attained his majority).

Chapter IV
Post-World War 1

After demobilisation

The last army pay slip amounted to £ 17 including a gratuity of £ 2. Sometime later, he received from the War Office a claim saying that he had been overpaid by the sum of 7/6 (7 shillings and 6 pence) and would he kindly repay it; Nick said he simply wrote back, marking on the slip "don't be bloody silly!" In 1929, he was awarded a small life pension[16].

Following his demobilisation, he entered the Singer Manufacturing Co Ltd factory at Clydebank and trained to be an engineer in textile machinery, going to night school as well as working as an apprentice, then as a Journeyman until his departure from the company on July 11, 1919. Destiny has it that a member of the family is again in the textile industry, this time in the midst of the use of industrial textile machinery on a large scale.

Moving to France to work with UWC

His reference from Singer is dated January 5, 1920, probably at the time he was in the process of obtaining employ with The Universal Winding Company of Boston – Leesona, (UWC) a textile machine manufacturer, based in the 10th arrondissement of Paris, which he joined on February 1, 1920. From Paris, the operations covered the whole of Europe and the Middle East.

---

[16] See annex for this pension.

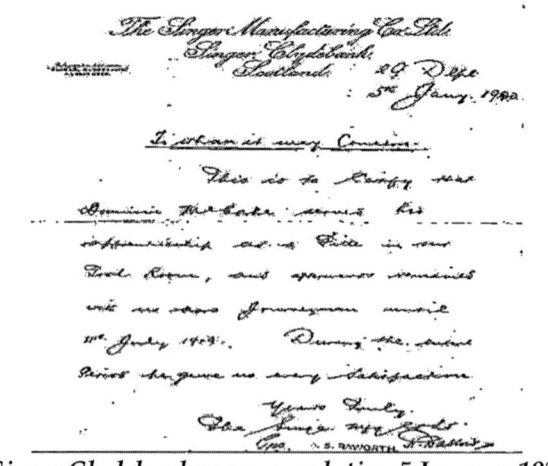

Singer Clydebank recommendation 5 January 1920

"*This is to certify that Dominic McCabe served his apprenticeship as a fitter in our Tool room and afterwards remained with us as a Journeyman until 11 July 1919. During the entire Period he gave us every satisfaction.*
Yours truly
The Singer Mfg Company Ltd.
Pps. A.S. RAWORTH"

I can imagine that for his new employer, The Universal Winding Company of Boston, also an American company, was well influenced by this recommendation in their search for a competent English-speaking engineer.

As mentioned previously, his sister, Mary, was already living in Nanterre, but it is not known what influence it had on his coming to France or residing in Nanterre. In 1920, Nick met my mother, Jeanne Louise Gastal, who also lived in Nanterre. They were engaged on December 18, 1920 and were married in Nanterre on September 10, 1921.

Dominic and Jeanne 1921

My parents' first child, Peter Edward, was born on November 1, 1922 at the Hertford British Hospital, 48 rue de Villiers, Levallois-Perret. His dark-auburn hair clearly showed the influence of the Celtic part of his descent of which, I am sure, Nick was very proud.

Nick and Peter

Travelling on business

In the course of his career with the Universal Winding Company, Nick was subjected to extensive travelling throughout Europe and the Middle East, notably Portugal, Holland, Belgium, Germany, Czechoslovakia, Romania, Bulgaria, Hungary, Greece, Turkey, Lebanon and perhaps other countries for which I cannot recall any indications, many witnessed by the hotel stickers glued to his leather suitcases or some copies of the UWC reports he wrote in his handsome, strong and stylish handwriting. As he was responsible for the installation of textile machines, he was obliged to stay away for several months in order to complete the projects. I know from my mother that this was the case of Portugal and also that he had a long spell in Erzerum in Turkey in 1934 installing the first textile machines there within Mustapha Kemal's industrial development programme.

Turkey, Erzerum Summer 1934 (Nick far right of the photo)

Nick appeared to like Portugal and Turkey and there are photos of him installing machines in Erzurum Turkey. He was amused by the way Turks fed pigeons with breadcrumbs dunked in raki and to see them afterwards staggering drunkenly. He spent some time in Constantinople (now Istanbul) and took photos there of the banks of the Bosphorous. No doubt, his thoughts then must have cast him back to almost twenty years when fighting in the Dardanelles when the aim was to capture Constantinople. I know from labels that had been stuck on one of his suitcases that he stayed at the "Divan Oteli" at Taksim and when I first visited Istanbul in 1964, I stayed in the same hotel. Unfortunately, they were unable to show me their records dating back to 1934.

From early on, my father loved the game of cricket, and during his long travels abroad, he would often take his cricket togs with him and address himself to the local British Embassy to try to get a game. From a letter I saw, I learnt that he joined the Caledonian Society of France in the year it was founded, 1922. Still functioning today, the society celebrated its 90th birthday in 2012. I also became a member of the society around 1960 and later in 2009/2010, I accepted to replace for one year the treasurer who had moved to the south of France.

Nick found Dresden, Prague and Budapest to be beautiful cities. He considered Czechoslovakia to be a highly advanced industrial country. His visits to Germany made him appreciate German efficiency especially at railway stations where smartly uniformed agents had a complete command of railway information when asked. He recalled that once, when buying postage stamps from a machine, the system went wrong and he pulled out an endless stream of stamps. It was during his missions there, and through his professional contacts that he learnt what was really going on in Germany, such as the setting up of concentration camps and the imprisonment for any kind of opposition detected towards the Nazi regime.

Nick often said that he did not like French bosses very much and I suppose he preferred to travel rather than spend time near them. He was very assiduous and at every voyage, he would write in his beautiful handwriting his reports to the Paris office, summing up the problems, raising technical question, making proposals for modifications and ordering replacement parts for customers.

Salaries for engineers at that time were not too high (probably the effects of the period of economic depression) and he was eager to put some money aside, so he would travel second-class on the railways and claim first class travel prices to which he was entitled. I don't think he ever travelled by aeroplane in those days, so considering the speed of trains at that time, travelling was tiring and uncomfortable and there was no returning home until the job was done.

He loved living in France and its way of life; he appreciated the wine and food and he often commented on the smallness of the kitchens in French flats and wondered how it was possible that the French housewife operating in such a limited space could come up with such marvellous dishes of food. He recognised the city of Lyons as being an extraordinary centre of gastronomy. In the summer, he took time for holidays with the family, going together to different parts of the Normandy coast each year and taking photos that are shown in the annex.

In the latter years of his career, due to his frequent visits to Greece, Turkey, the Lebanon and Portugal, all having hot climates, he insisted that the firm pay for his summer clothes, some being beautifully tailored in Greece. One suit was off-white made of silk and linen, and another was a black pin stripe suite that later I wore in my early days working for the Norwich Union in Brighton.

The darkening clouds menacing war spreading from Germany to the rest of Europe and what he himself witnessed in Germany led to a great extent to Dominic's decision to return to Britain. It was in 1937 that he decided that it would be best for him and his family to return to the UK and he intimated this to U W C near the end of that year. He wrote from Hotel Xenias Melathron in Athens on January 14, 1938 to the Paris office that he had received no news from the company regarding his intention to settle in Great Britain. Nick indicated that he was willing to continue working for the company while domiciled in England, but he felt obliged to leave France before the end of 1938. Following the preparations for the move, our family left France in September that year. The leaving certificate issued by the Paris office management of Universal Winding

Company dated March 31, 1938 was very praiseworthy of Nick's professional achievements.

Apart from the major reason, the political situation, there were also several other considerations for his wishing to return to the UK. First of all, from a political point of view, during his professional visits to Germany, he observed the rising strength of Hitler's Nazi Party and the treatment of Jews and of German opponents all considered to be Bolsheviks whether that was true or not. He regretted the lack of reaction to the remilitarisation of the Ruhr in 1936 and he said that "it only needed to have a British Officer and a squadron of French soldiers sent there to stop Hitler at that time" (certainly true in this very British formulation!). The Anschluss, annexation of Austria by Germany took place in March 1938. It was clear to him that Germany was preparing to invade France. He sometimes said that one had to be a politician not to see that Germany would make war and invade France. As a Scot, a British citizen, he knew that if he stayed in France, the Germans, at best, would intern him. As it turned out, a month after his return to Great Britain, Adolf Hitler's army marched into the Sudetenland in Czechoslovakia on October 1, 1938, representing clearly what would unfold in the future.

His health had taken its toll due to the First World War and to his profession requiring extensive travelling in somewhat difficult climates and conditions. It is not hard to imagine that long absences from home spoiled family life. Nick was not too happy with the local French management of the Paris office and he aspired to have more freedom. It so happened that his sister "Dolla" who lived in Brighton had lost her husband, Gillie, who had developed tuberculosis. He was a Scottish Legal Life Insurance agent and it presented an opportunity for Nick to take over from his sister her late husband's portfolio thus giving "Dolla" a certain income.

Chapter V
Return to Great Britain

Arrival in Brighton

We arrived in England in September 1938 after taking the train in Paris at the Gare St Lazare for Dieppe where we boarded the boat for Newhaven. I still remember saying goodbye on the train, probably to my aunts. When we arrived in Brighton, we lodged temporarily at my Aunt Dolla's flat at 98 Buckingham Road.

After leaving Aunt Dolla's flat, our first home was a requisitioned flat at 53 Dyke Road just before the Seven Dials roundabout. We had no furniture of our own and Nick bought excellent second-hand furniture in the Brighton Lanes. We had a Kilim carpet that Nick had brought back from Turkey and antique Asian plates for decorating the walls. I went to Stanford Road School that was some way further on the other side of the Seven Dials.

Behind our flat, we overlooked the glass roof of the garage situated below with a view towards the east where the Brighton railway station lay in the valley with the lines directed towards London and the north, as well as the south east coast. Next door in the street, there was baker's shop where we would buy our loaf of bread (no baguette then!). I recall that our next-door neighbours were Mr and Mrs Sawyer (Elise) and I was told that they were vegetarians. As a small boy, I understood that they only ate vegetables and not meat, but to me, it seemed strange and that they must be a bit particular in their ways and not like other people.

There was no position vacant for Nick as an engineer in his former company's subsidiary (Universal Winding Company) based in Manchester and in any case, he wished to be free and independent. During 1938 and 1939, he corresponded with R.J. Schilling, representative of the Universal Winding Company who was then based in Basel, Switzerland. There is no trace of what Nick wrote but there are four letters and a telegram from Mr Schilling which are informative not only on some of the affairs of UWC, but also on the evolution of the political situation in continental Europe in the light of the growing power of the Nazi regime in Germany and Austria[17]. Regarding the Nazi take-over of Czechoslovakia that commenced in the Sudetenland in October 1938, I recall Nick saying later what a highly developed industrial country Czechoslovakia was at that time and that Britain should never had allowed Germany to invade that country.

In his new situation in England, as already mentioned Nick, made an arrangement to take over the Scottish Legal Life Insurance portfolio of Dolla's deceased husband. It was Industrial Life Insurance involving weekly, or otherwise regular (weekly or monthly) door-to-door collection of small premiums from the insured: 6d (6 pence), 1/- (a shilling), 1/6d, or 2/-, at a time. I remember often seeing on his desk the ledger which contained many columns of pounds, shillings and pence (£ s d), full of figures which had to be totted up, balanced by page and carried forward to the next one. In order to cover his clientele in such a large, hilly town as Brighton, he bought a BSA motorcycle.

Nick liked the freedom that the job accorded him and to be outside and to be in contact with people. In the summer, it enabled him to take time to see cricket matches at the Sussex County Cricket Club of which he was a member. He read with much pleasure articles on cricket matches published in the Daily Telegraph.

---

[17] See annex for the content of the Schiller letters.

Brighton, May 7, 1939

The 2ⁿᵈ World War

I clearly recall the day in September 3, 1939 when on the BBC one o'clock (1 pm) news, Mr Chamberlain (the Prime Minister) made a statement confirming the declaration of war on Germany following the Nazi invasion of Poland. As from July 1940, after mines were laid and barbed wire installed, the Brighton and Hove beaches were closed off from the public. We could then no longer descend to the lower promenade, level with the beach, whereas we could still walk past anti-aircraft guns that were stationed at regular intervals on the upper promenade at street level. These weapons, surrounded by walls of sandbags, were pointed at the sky overlooking the sea in the Channel separating us from enemy occupied Europe from whence enemy aircraft could now launch air attacks.

Brighton and Hove seafront cordoned off from the beach in 1940[18]

Following Neville Chamberlain's resignation, Winston Churchill was appointed Prime Minister who immediately went about organising Great Britain to ensure its defence and to wage a long war. From then on, he never ceased to bolster the population's courage through his actions and particularly his regular speeches broadcast on the radio and in parliament. I remember listening to the BBC with my parents and although I was still quite young, I was very impressed by the tone and words spoken by Churchill and his speeches gave courage to the nation despite brutal air raid attacks on the country and he conveyed his resolution to win the war by rallying Britain's allies, members of the then British Empire abroad, and the United States to "give us the tools and we'll finish the job"! His well-chosen words were most moving and important especially when having to overcome early setbacks in the war. Whereas, the British broadcasts abroad were jammed by Germany, we could capture some of Hitler's vociferations on the radio, and for Nick who had some understanding of the German language, the malignant and fascist nature of the Nazi propaganda came out very clearly.

At that time, we didn't have television, of course, but the radio provided many good programmes. I can say that it formed my ear to classical music for life, many of the programmes I listened to were concerts of great composers, predominantly the German and Austrian ones, Bach, Beethoven, Brahms, Haendel, Haydn, Mozart, Schubert, etc. It formed my musical taste for the rest of my life. The war with Germany was not an obstacle to our appreciating Germany's cultural past. There

---

[18] Source: thanks to Royal Pavilion and Museum; Brighton and Hove Licence CC BY-SA

were also theatre plays such as the Forsyth Saga, and adventure stories like The Saint. To keep the morale of the nation in good spirits many comedies were broadcast ridiculing the Nazis like ITMA, "It's that Man again" with Tommy Handley, "Workers' Playtime" and also musicals with Vera Lynn singing moving songs referring to the boys doing their military service and giving everyone hope. A series of Gilbert and Sullivan light operas like "The Pirates of Penzance", were also broadcast.

Nick who had fought as a soldier in World War I, despite misgivings on the way that conflict had been run, remained a man with a sense of duty to his country and he now volunteered as an Air Raid Warden in the civil defence organisation called Air Raid Precautions the A.R.P., already set up in 1935, and besides his gas mask he was equipped with a black helmet bearing these initials.

It was in the summer of 1940 that the German army overran northern France and the subsequent fall of Paris was a cause of great distress, not only to my mother, but also to my father who appreciated life in France, which had become his home.

My brother, Douglas, who was nearly thirteen years old when we left France in 1938, had not been prepared in France for studying in English, and he had difficulties in his schooling at the Xaverian College, Brighton. Fortunately, through the kind father of one of his schoolmates, he got a job at Lloyds Insurance Brokers in London when he was 14/15 years old. It seems that there had been some conflicts between Nick and Douglas, but I was too small to understand what it was all about. Probably growing adolescence differing with the older generation coupled with aggravation on the part of Nick due to a decline in his health (he was later operated for duodenal ulcer which had caused him considerable pain). As a result of this and the difference in age between us (Douglas was eight years older than I), we never spent too much time together and so I was used to being alone with my parents and left to my own devices for occupying my time.

When Douglas was 17, he faked his age and joined the Royal Navy. I was very proud of him. His early missions were devoted to accompanying convoys taking equipment to Soviet Russia after Hitler had attacked the country. Once he was on leave with us at Dyke Road in Brighton, and I shall always remember the event. There was suddenly a great noise of aircraft above our heads and looking out of the window of my bedroom on the street side of the flat, I distinctly saw the faces of the pilots of two out of three Messerschmitt planes, which were heading for the railway. My brother whisked me under the bed to protect me against the effect of a bomb that might be coming our way. My mother very rashly ran to the rear side of the flat in the kitchen and looking through the open door on a small balcony, she saw a bomb launched. The outside door banged and closed and luckily, the "black-out curtain" unrolled itself and protected her from the slivers of glass of the door blasted by the explosion of the bomb. The lady in the same position in the flat below was not as fortunate, as she received glass in her head and eventually lost the sight of one eye.

It was near lunchtime and soon, Nick arrived on his motorbike that he gingerly guided over the broken glass of the garage roof when parking his vehicle. He immediately put on his ARP Warden's helmet and went straight to a nearby building, Buckingham Court, where the bomb fell, the railway line having been missed. With other helpers, inhabitants were guided out of the debris and Nick luckily escaped from a falling wall as he stepped out. That evening we housed a couple, Mr and Mrs Fox who stayed with us for a fortnight while awaiting accommodation. I recall Nick often pacing up and down the corridor at night in pain from his duodenal ulcer. On June 9, 1942, my father entered the Sussex County Hospital and was operated for a duodenal ulcer on the 22nd and he returned home at Dyke Road on July 8. It granted him relief from suffering for some years. He smoked regularly and I profited from the series of cigarette cards[19] that were contained in the cigarette packets, many of them being "Wills Woodbines".

Sometime later, we moved to 12 Clifton Terrace branching off Dyke Road leading towards the town centre and the sea. It was a private house owned by Mrs Adams, a war widow of an officer of the Royal Navy. We had the two upper floors of the house and as we were on a hill, we had a beautiful view looking out towards the sea.

In front of the house, there was a residential garden for this street's inhabitants. I soon made friends with a few children in this place and we had a happy time playing all sorts of games. In this very discreet area, two separate constructions were built at a distance from each other in the gardens. One was a Nissen hut surrounded by thick mortar bricks and housed a reserve of weapons and ammunition of all sorts for defence purposes. Fenced off was the other one-storey building, a First Aid medical unit where we could get our cuts and bruises attended to and its purpose of course was to serve in case of general emergency.

Assistance from the countries of the British Empire (later to become the Commonwealth countries) brought us food among other things, and enabled the distribution of milk in the schools, as well as cod liver oil, egg powder, powdered chocolate, etc. Our dependence on imported food

---

[19] The series of cigarette cards treated various subjects like motorcars, motorcycles, regimental army uniforms, household hints, etc.

was assured by naval convoys at risk from German U boat attacks and led to a "Dig for Victory" campaign in Britain to use part of such garden amenities. So we were allotted a space and I enjoyed helping Nick to plant all sorts of vegetables, such as: tomatoes, runner beans, carrots, potatoes, radishes, turnips, peas, cabbages, leeks and also marrows which grew on a compost heap set up by Nick against the fence mentioned above and regularly fuelled by vegetable peelings, eggshells and other degradable matter.

With a view to encourage savings of all kinds in a difficult economic situation requiring a concentration of efforts and resources to produce the needs for winning the war, many slogans were devised besides "Dig for Victory", such as: "Waste not, want not!", "Is your journey really necessary?", "Switch off that light!", "Make do and mend!", "Lend a hand on the land", "Coughs and sneezes spread diseases!", "Keep calm and carry on!", as for security: "Loose talk can cost lives!".

For Nick, it was a great pleasure to be outside in the open-air gardening and to see the fruits of his labour in the allotment. Unfortunately, his health was not good, and he was often away for treatment. One night when he was away in hospital, I was alone with my mother during an air raid warning and we heard a big explosion and then the noise of bullets being fired continuously. We had to go down to the cellar of Mrs Adams until the "all clear" sounded. A Messerschmitt plane had been shot down in a graveyard very close to us, and it was its ammunition that the fire had set off that explained the shots. One German airman was found strung up with his parachute in a nearby tree, whereas the other pilot had parachuted down to the beach. I still remember clearly the smell of the burnt fuselage when I passed by the graveyard the next day.

My mother had to go to hospital at the Brighton Municipal on November 14, 1944 for an operation on the 22nd and returned home at Clifton Terrace three weeks later. I remember D-day. After it was announced, I went up to a top floor room where there was a skylight. There had been a storm in the night, but in the morning, the sun was shining. I climbed on to a chair to look out westwards through the open skylight hoping to see as far as the Isle of Wight the naval activity crossing the Channel, but of course, it was too far away. Later on, when Douglas came on leave, we learnt that he had been near the Isle of Wight area preparing for the D-Day invasion working on the fitting up of barrage balloons to impede approaches and attacks by enemy aircraft to landing craft being made ready. He brought home bits and pieces of the material making the balloons, on the outside a sort of silver-coloured, sturdy, rubbery, expandable material with cotton fabric on the inside. He also brought with him a few goodies in the way of chewing gum and chocolate given by the Americans stationed near his unit.

At the first Christmas after D-Day (1944), my father managed to get hold of a wonderful bottle of Pommard (Burgundy wine) that a pub had in its cellar from before the war. It was my first taste of good wine (but not the last!) and I have never forgotten its taste. It accompanied a turkey that year well prepared by my mother. I recall that the next year we had a goose for the Christmas lunch (an even better meal) also accompanied by a bottle of Burgundy wine that I believe was a Beaune or a Beaune Villages.

When the war in Europe ended a year later, somehow my Great-Aunt, Tante Jeanne, or my mother managed to get hold of a French Flag that we proudly hung out of our window. I also remember that at the Brighton War Memorial at Old Steine Nick attended a victory ceremony with the British Legion.

Sometime later, Aunt Mary, my father's sister who had remained living in Nanterre, France, during the whole conflict, came over to Britain for a visit. I was then eleven years old and fascinated by some of my father's war souvenirs, consisting mainly of: a colonial helmet which I found very smart, a pair of binoculars (not sure if these were of military origin), an enormous pistol far too heavy for my small hands, and a rifle. When I gleefully showed this last item to Aunt Mary, she was very upset and informed me that she had lost a son, resisting the German invasion. I discovered during the past few years of research that he was Oswald Harold André BUCHARDT, a soldier in the « 117ème Régiment d'Infantrie », killed on June 10, 1940, at Neuilly-Saint-Front in the Aisne Department, Champagne area. The military authorities officially recognised his death in the terms of « Mort pour la France » and his name is inscribed on the 2nd World War Memorial of his hometown Nanterre. Next to this stands the 1st World War Memorial where Jeanne's brother, Edouard GASTAL, has his name inscribed having been killed on March 25, 1918 in the Somme. So, in the Nanterre memorial park, two young men of French/Scottish/Danish origins meet here having laid down their lives in two world wars and later they have something in common familywise.

Peacetime

At the end of the war, we were moved to Montpelier Road, the part below the Western Road and not far from the sea. I believe that it was formerly a hotel that had been requisitioned. We lived there until we were relocated in a semi-detached house built in a newly established council estate at Coldean at the northern edge of Brighton.

It was after our move to Montpelier Road in 1945 that my father decided to send me to the Xaverian College, the same Roman Catholic day school my brother, Douglas, had attended. The College was run by a teaching order, the Xaverian Brothers and I started in Form 2. I used to take a bus to get there as it was quite far away from where we lived. Occasionally, I would walk there to save a bit of bus fare for pocket money.

Due to his Irish origins, Nick was a Roman Catholic and he was brought up as such and it explains his choice of schooling for Douglas and me. My mother was of the Protestant faith due to the origins of her grandfather, Jules Jacques Combe born in Switzerland. A member of that family had in fact been a Protestant pastor in Vevey, Canton de Vaud. This difference of religious faith never caused the slightest conflict or problem. I lived in a very peaceful atmosphere and I cannot recall at any time any kind of dispute between my parents in my presence. Nick appreciated Jeanne's culinary talents and when a good meat dish was served, he would say "it's tender as a husband's love!" which provoked a quizzical smile and laughter from Jeanne. Although I never saw my father do any cooking, he did make pots of yoghurt that were covered while they were warm and placed on a sort of tray on the top of a cupboard. It was a custom to eat yoghurt in Turkey and after the First World War, it became popular in France.

I was quite happy at home; I was never spoilt by gifts and quite content with the few toys I had (a few aluminium French toy soldiers my brother brought with him from France plus some toy soldiers and several wooden bricks which I used for building imaginary fortresses).

Our home was pleasantly furnished with taste and good quality second-hand furniture my father had bought in the Lanes in Brighton after our arrival from France. Among other things, we had leather bound armchairs and a sofa as well as a Turkish Kilim carpet my father had brought back from his travels. We had an extensible dining room table with chairs and a buffet in which there was table linen and dining room cutlery and porcelain. In one of the drawers, my father kept a big heavy revolver, probably war booty (only officers were armed with revolvers). Generally, kitchens were large in England and we had sufficient space to eat in ours during the week.

Nick used the traditional long bladed razor for shaving daily and I was always dead scared when seeing him with his quick strokes wipe off the lather from the razor on to his bare arm. I never saw him ever use a safety razor like my brother did.

We had a mixture of books at home, French and English. Nick was fascinated by astronomy and liked reading Jeans on astronomy. He admired T. E. Lawrence's work, such as "The Seven Pillars of Wisdom", Rudyard Kipling's the "1st and 2nd Jungle Book" contemporary to his epoch, also books by John Buchan. There were also two editions of "Punch" July to December 1914 and January to June 1915. I used to spend hours on the carpet going through these, absorbing the caricatures of the European Politicians of the times as well the amusing cartoons displaying the way people dressed, spoke and lived during these early war years. The French books were classical literature with, of course, the 1937 "Petit Larousse" dictionary that had a wealth of information and several sepia photos of paintings and sculptures in the Louvre. It helped to form my sense of aesthetics and my attachment to French culture and history in my early years.

Below our flat at Montpellier Road lived a very pleasant couple, John and Ida Coak with two children, Sheila and David and we became close friends. Ida was good company for Jeanne in the daytime and we often had good laughs when we were all together. When we left to live in Coldean, Ida had fallen ill and later in 1961, we learnt that she died of breast cancer. I have kept the correspondence of that time because we had lived unforgettable moments of joy and cordiality together in those days.

I was very free to go out on my own as long as I was back at the time requested by my parents. I often went to the beach in summer and I liked to go to the shops like Woolworths along the Western Road to see if there were some toy soldiers, not too expensive to add to my small collection. I liked going down Preston Street where there was a very good toyshop where I would gaze at the shop window to see the latest novelties which I never dared believe I would have some day, but it was not a problem. As I grew older, I walked miles to go from one of the numerous parks in Brighton and Hove to another and to get a game of cricket or football with chums I met.

With my father, "Nick", on December 26, 1945 at East Brighton

I was very independent, and I liked moving around discovering new places; distance was never an obstacle. As time went by and my schoolwork became more important, no one at home was ever on my back and I was left to get on with it. With hindsight, I wish I had had more pressure to do better, but my father was sometimes away for medical treatment and at some days of the week, he would see clients who were only available in the evening. My school marks were good, and I was placed in the top four or five but as for my Oxford School Certificate exams in 1950, although the results were satisfactory, I feel that I could have done better.

It was in that year, before the final exams that my school organised the Sports Day. I was very happy because my father attended the occasion. Nick was able to play cricket there, that day, in a match organised for the fathers of the students. I was the captain of Campion House that won the competition against the other three houses, and at the same time, I won the Victor Ludorum cup. After the athletics, there was a cricket match organised for the parents (meaning the fathers), and it pleased me to see Nick play the sport he liked the best. A few days later, he came home with a few copies of the Evening Argus, the local newspaper, which contained a small article about my performance on our Sports Day entitled "A Coming Wooderson" (a former world record holder for the "mile") mentioning my winning several events and for which Nick was proud.

Winning the 440 yards – Sports Day June 1950

Nick started complaining of pains in the chest in 1950. For this, he was admitted to the Sussex County Hospital, Brighton, on September 20, 1950 and returned home on November 2. In March 1951, he was sent to Robertsbridge Sanatorium, Sussex, and stayed there for about two years. On October 29, 1953, my father entered St Georges Hospital in London to be operated on November 5 for collapsing his left lung. On November 26, he went to Atkinson Morlay Hospital, Copse Hill, Wimbledon, London, SW 20 for convalescence until December 11 when he returned home at Coldean, Brighton.

During this period, I was doing my Military Service (June 5, 1952–June 4, 1954) the last part at the Joint Services School for Languages at Bodmin in Cornwall[20] and I came home for Christmas 1953. Later after my return to camp, I applied for a "Compassionate Posting" at home in

---

[20] Owing to the « Cold War" the Russian language was taught there to the three arms, but I was simply in the logistics section.

view of Nick's condition that had become so serious. Unfortunately, after a short respite, Nick had to return to St Georges Hospital on March 4, 1954 when doctors operated again. I remember walking with him on the way home just after his operation and he said he was better now and looking forward to watching cricket matches again in the summer. In fact, the doctors had discovered that he had advanced lung cancer. This I learned later when I visited our family doctor, Dr Lindeck who explained to me the true situation. Soon after Nick found himself paralysed from the waist downwards. In those times, there was not much transparency of information with patients by the medical profession. Dr Lindeck estimated that he only had two months to live. Undoubtedly, his smoking cigarettes contributed to the development of his lung cancer for which there was not much public warning on this danger at that time.

Due to his paralysis, it was most difficult to care for him at home and he was then hospitalised in the Sussex General Hospital. His ordeal lasted four months and during that time, he still expressed hopes of getting better and watching cricket again. On July 19, 1954, my mother and Aunt Dolla were at his bedside when he died around 6 pm. I had left earlier to eat a meal at my girlfriend's house and on my return to the hospital I met my mother and my aunt walking down the hill of Elm Grove and they announced the news. They said that I could still go to see him, but I declined because I did not want to have uppermost in mind the picture of his emaciated and disfigured face caused by his illness.

My brother, Douglas, who lived in London at that time, came home. The funeral service took place at St Joseph's Church at the bottom of Elm Grove. Sidney King who had done all kinds of jobs in his life, be it carrying sacks of coal or being a waiter, was handsomely dressed and he escorted my mother. He was of great comfort and a perfect gentleman. Some of my school friends also attended. The burial took place in the cemetery at the top of Bear Road on the left-hand side going up the hill.

Thoughts about my father "Nick"

"Nick" was a self-made man, who had a modest family background, but he worked hard to become a textile engineer through apprenticeship and also thanks to the educational opportunities open to him in Glasgow by way of night school. He acquired much of his culture since living in France as from 1920, speaking the French language well and acquiring some knowledge of German and always reading during the spare moments afforded by constant travel. I have always appreciated the fact that despite his professional and cultural promotion, he never turned his back on his family origins and always remained a strong supporter of the working classes.

He was a handsome man, well-mannered, well-dressed when the occasion required it and of good bearing. But in my last recollection of him, his face was lined after many years of suffering. In looking back on what I know of his life, I realise that the suffering written on his face was both moral and physical.

The suffering that I have mentioned can be partly attributed to the horrors of the First World War, which he experienced on two war fronts between the summer of 1915, at Gallipoli, in the Dardanelles, Turkey, and then in the winter of 1917 at the Somme in France. His early physical wellbeing was affected by dysentery contracted in Gallipoli, bringing him back home in October 1915. After his convalescence in Scotland, on January 2, 1917, he was sent to the French front "La Somme", where he suffered frostbite, some gas attacks, shrapnel injuries and also long periods of duty in water-filled trenches before being returned to hospital care in March 1917, this time in Lancashire. He was invalided out in April 1918 and qualified for a small pension. Apart from the fatigue from tiresome conditions of travelling in his profession, in 1930 on March 24, my parents suffered the tragic loss of their first son, Peter who died of meningitis, at the age of seven in dire circumstances, such that Nick prevented Jeanne from witnessing the final outcome.

When I finished school in 1950, at the age of 16, Nick got me my first job with the Norwich Union Insurance Co. in Brighton. It was difficult to realise that I would have to wait at least 40 years to have prolonged summer holidays again, as when I was a schoolboy! As I progressed, I was transferred to the St James Street branch in London and commuted daily by train.

Nick left some most interesting records of poems, drawings and photos collected essentially from his fellow soldier patients and nurses from October 1915 until the autumn of 1916. There are also, between former colleagues in the company he worked for, the exchange of a few enlightening letters about the drama that was taking place in Europe in the period prior to the outbreak of the Second World War.

Chapter VI
My Mother Jeanne and Her Family

Jules Jacques Combe

My mother's ancestors, on her mother's side (Combe), are traced way back to before 1380 in the person of Jean de Comba at Orbe, Vaud, in Switzerland. He was a notary from 1382 to 1413 and a Councillor in 1396. A genealogical tree from that period until 1872 has been handed down.

Jules Jacques Combe, my other's grandfather, was born at Morges, Vaud, Switzerland, on March 16, 1837. At the age of 25, he became the tutor to the children of the Grand Duke Heir of Saxe Weimar[21] at Heidelberg until 1864. He taught them French and most likely German and English which he had mastered. His mission appears to have been well appreciated and following an exchange of correspondence many years later regarding a reference, he asked for to enable him to teach German, the Grand Duke Charles August readily and warmly wrote to him in perfect French on July 4, 1880. It is interesting to note that the troubled times (war between France and the Prussians in 1870) which had occurred during the lapse of time since his departure in 1864 and the date of this letter[22]. Good human relations unspoiled!

After his tutorship in Germany, Jules then settled in the Brussels area. He founded there a printing business and was a translator of German, English and French. He married Lucie Delaroyère, French, born at Hazelbrouck, in northern France. In 1872, Lucie gave birth to Juliette who later became the mother of Jeanne my mother. Jules Combe's mother died in July 1876 just before the birth of his second daughter Jeanne Jacqueline (my mother's "Tante Jeanne") On August 5. A letter dated July 17 from Jules' father, Jacques, a Protestant minister at Orbe, Switzerland, recounts the last moments of his wife, Jeanne (née Chatelanat) and makes

---

[21] See Annex for copy of certificate N° 4772 established February 12, 1864 by Grand Duke's administration.

[22] See Annex for copy of letter from the Grand Duke dated July 4, 1880 giving J.J. Combe a recommendation.

reference to the forthcoming birth of Jules's second daughter Jeanne Jacqueline.

Later, he moved to France at Nanterre on the western side of Paris. On one of his letters dated July 8, 1906, the paper heading shows:

J. COMBE Ingénieur, Membre de la Société des Imprimeurs civils de France.
Traducteur Technique d'Allemand et d'Anglais.
23 rue du Docteur-Foucault, Nanterre.

I discovered at the BNF (Bibliothèque Nationale de France), that it as Jules Jacques Combe who had translated Andrew Carnegie's book, "Triumphant Democracy", into French: "Le Triomphe de la Démocratie" edited by E. Dentu, publisher in Paris in 1886. I visited Dunfermline in 2008 and learned the merits of Andrew Carnegie, quite ignorant at that time of the above fact implicating my great grandfather.

He left writings of a stories and correspondence exchanged with his younger daughter Jeanne Jacqueline (my great-aunt, Tante Jeanne), who had studied in Germany before becoming a teacher of French in several Girls' High Schools in England. His letters to her demonstrate his great qualities as a pedagogue.

With regard to his writing, aside from his correspondence with his family, he wrote some stories and the text for a pictorial story. In a letter of 1896 addressed to his daughter Jeanne Jacqueline ("Tante Jeanne"), Jules Jacques explains that he had traced from the newspaper, "Le Figaro", thirteen drawings on the theme "The Creation of the Bicycle"[23], stating that they were drawn by "Caran d'Ache", a famous illustrator for this newspaper. In fact, Jules traced copies of these drawings and invented the text for each tableau that he signs as being by "Bibi"[24] calling this work a "drama". In his presentation, he states that the well-known General Poillouë de Saint-Mars had said, "The bicycle is a marvellous machine that is ideal… Its motor is just the human leg that seems to have been expressly created for the pedal." Jules' explanations in this letter demonstrate how meticulous he was in his research and in his way of doing things, even the choice of colour of the inks according to the purpose of their use.

---

[23] **See annex** for the drawings and the text translated into English for the "drama" of **"The Creation of the Bicycle".** I have now established that the "Bibliothèque Nationale de France" has the original drawings by Caran d'Ache published in the Figaro.

[24] « Bibi » is a French term meaning "myself".

When taking long walks with the young children, he noticed that halfway through the children became tired and restless. Carrying one on his back made him tired, without solving the problem, so he would sometimes start to tell a story to distract them and they enjoyed it to an extent that at each outing they would arrive home peacefully and content and then claim a new tale. He thus resorted to drawing a picture of himself leading the children up a hill and wrote down in his impeccable handwriting a serial story a story called "Voyages de Jules Hiver sur la planète Vénus" ("Voyages of Jules Hiver (winter) on the planet Venus")[25]. There is subtlety in choosing the title "Jules Hiver" because it sounds very much like "Gulliver" as if in French the "G" was soft, although when followed by a "u" it is in fact hard in pronunciation. I see no other reason for adjoining "Hiver" in the title of the story. As for the tale, it describes, with humour, an attempt, with the aid of a hot air balloon (« une Montgolfière ») to rise as far as possible in the atmosphere with the aim of approaching more closely the sight of the planet Venus. He cleverly explains all the technical details of the preparation for this venture assisted by a professional astronaut who at the last minute accidentally and amusingly drops off the balloon, detaching the last connections attached to the ground and leaving Jules Hiver to his own devices in the ascending aircraft. Naturally, as it can be expected, he copes with the situation!

In a book published in Vienna in 1931, "Die Photographische Kamera und ihr Zubehör" (The photographic camera and its accessories) mention in German is made of Jules Jacques' contribution in 1928 in the following statement: 'For the sake of completeness, JULES JACQUES COMBE in Nanterre (Seine) in 1928 has suggested that the front wall of the hole camera be provided with several holes; The holes are arranged one above the other, can be closed and can be used as required. The purpose of the device is to make recordings of high objects (D.R. 108. 556).'

It is clear that Jules Combe had an important cultural influence on the family due to his writings and knowledge of German and English in addition to French. This can be seen in the exchange of letters with his unmarried daughter, Jeanne Jacqueline ("Tante Jeanne"). Reading French literature was a great pastime of my mother and her sisters and they never ceased writing regularly to each other.

---

[25] See copy in the annex.

Juliette Combe, Jules Combe's eldest daughter, (my Grandmother)

Juliette (Juliette, Georgine, Henriette, Elise, Emilie) Combe, the elder daughter of Jules Jacques Combe, born December 26, 1872, had married Henri (Henri, René, Georges) Gastal on May 1, 1895 at Nanterre. The "Livret de Famille" indicates that Henri was an Insurance Clerk. Three weeks before the birth of my mother, Jeanne Louise, Juliette wrote to her sister, Jeanne Jacqueline, to say "dans un mois tu seras Tante" ("in a month's time, you will be an aunt") [26]. Jeanne Louise was born in Nanterre on February 19, 1896 and was the eldest of nine children.

Jeanne's brothers and sisters were: Edouard (called "Doudou") born March 23, 1897; Georges (called "Titi") born September 23, 1898; Jacques born July 5, 1900; Cécile born October 24, 1901; Madeleine born December 30, 1906; René born June 28, 1908; Hubert born December 28, 1909; Yvonne born March 12, 1911.

Juliette's health suffered from her numerous childbirths, the loss, not only of her husband, Henri, who in his 52nd year, died on November 19, 1917, but also that of her eldest son, Edouard who was killed as a soldier in the war on March 25, 1918 in the Somme. In July 1928, she went to the north of France, at Bertrancourt, in the Somme department, to rest as she was in a very weak condition. She wrote from there to her sister, Jeanne Jacqueline "Tante Jeanne" on July 15, 1928 giving her news and thanking her for sending two books to read[27]. She died there three months later on October 16, in her 56th year.

Jeanne Jacqueline, Jules Combe's second daughter, my Great Aunt ("Tante Jeanne" – my mother's Aunt)

Tante Jeanne was born in Brussels on August 5, 1876 and was baptised at the Brussels Evangelical Church of the Museum. Like her father, Jules Jacques, her nationality was Swiss (later, when she settled in Great Britain, she was naturalised British).

---

[26] See copy of Juliette's letter dated January 26, 1896.

[27] See copy of Juliette's letter dated July 15, 1928 written just after her arrival at Bertrancourt and addressed to her sister, Jeanne Jacqueline "Tante Jeanne".

Tante Jeanne, on the left, with her sister Juliette, mother of Jeanne Louise

I learned from the correspondence between her and her father, that after her family had settled in Nanterre, at the age of 18 she was in a small private school. According to Tante Jeanne's handwritten notes, and the records of the Teachers Registration Council (London), she was at Neston, Cheshire, England from 1898 to 1901. From 1901 until 1906, she taught, as Second French Mistress, at Redland High School for Girls in Bristol. In 1906, she went to Frankfurt-on-Main in Germany, until 1908. On her return, she taught French at Surbiton High School, Kingston-on-Thames from 1908 until 1913. In that year, she joined Wolverhampton Girls' High School as Senior French Mistress and remained there until 1920. Tante Jeanne then went to teach at Kesteven and Grantham Girls' School in Lincolnshire in 1920 until 1924 when, as French Mistress, she joined Colston's Girls' School in Bristol. A year later, she entered the High School at Bedford for her longest and last teaching appointment that ended in 1936 when she retired.

During her retirement, she lived in a boarding house at Hove and I sometimes visited her, and we played an ancient card game "Bézigue" that we found very amusing. Tante Jeanne came regularly to visit us in the daytime for lunch followed by the ritual of taking coffee around the coffee table covered by a circular tablecloth embroidered with colourful anemones. Old Combe family silverware, a sugar bowl (engraved with the date of 1850 "Souvenir"), a small, silver, milk jug and small, coffee spoons were set out. Jeanne ground the coffee beans in the wooden manual grinder and used an aluminium percolator for making the coffee. Sometimes Tante Jeanne would drink a small glass of cognac and dip a lump of sugar in it and give it to me as a "petit canard" as she called it.

Jeanne Louise Gastal, my Mother "Jeanne"

I know little of my mother's childhood, except that as the eldest, she helped her mother to look after her brothers and sisters when growing up. She had blue eyes and blonde hair, a charming little brown wart below her right eye and one front tooth slightly overlapping the other, far from it being horrific, as it may sound, her face was beautifully attractive. During all her life, she always had a ready smile when approached.

Jeanne Louise with her three sisters and her five brothers

She went to England as a « gouvernante » ("au pair" girl) in an English family (Warren) at Bristol during the First World War. Later, she worked in the offices of the American Express in rue Scribe, Paris. She thus acquired a good knowledge of English while maintaining during her life a delightful French accent when she spoke.

Jeanne Louise Gastal – July 1919

Mr Warren of Bristol and his son who was killed in the 1914 War

Jeanne met Dominick in Nanterre in 1920. It is unknown to me how they were introduced. Nick's sister, Mary lived in Nanterre since about 1910, married to a Dane, Buchardt. Did she know Jeanne before Nick arrived in France? Obviously, because Jeanne had lived in England during the early part of the 1st World War and had learnt to speak in English, communication between them was facilitated. It should be remembered also that they each had a common loss of a brother in the First World War that was certainly a subject of conversation between them. In a small, red leather-bound Universal Winding Company notebook given by Nick, my mother inscribed several notes in her beautiful handwriting. She wrote that on the December 18, 1920 she was engaged « avec Mon Cher et adorable Nick », also that on December 25, Nick offered her a beautiful handbag[28]. On February 14 (St Valentine Day) the following year, Nick had to leave for Belfort, and beforehand he gave her a pair of gloves for her birthday that fell on February 19. They were married in Nanterre on September 10, 1921.

Jeanne, Peter and Dominic ("Nick"), November 1922

---

[28] See annex for copy of these comments.

As previously mentioned, Jeanne's first child, Peter, was born on November 1, 1922, Jeanne's second child, Douglas was born on December 1, 1925. Peter's school exercise book for the period October to December 1929 has survived in our archives and shows good marks obtained in his class. Tragically, on March 24, 1930 Peter died of meningitis, it was such a great loss in terrible circumstances causing of course distress for all three remaining members of the family, my mother's first baby, also for my father seeing the effect of the disease causing the death of his first son and forbidding Jeanne to witness the horror of the outcome of this illness. It was tragic also for my brother who lost the happy companionship of his elder brother. The date of my birth on March 24, 1934, was a terrible coincidence that I discovered only in my adolescence when looking through the "Livret de Famille", an official document issued to couples upon marriage registering the marriage and the births and deaths as they occurred.

Nick's work led him to be often absent abroad and Jeanne was often alone with her children. Of course, Nick was working in the UWC's offices in Paris between business trips and was able to enjoy family life. It was the summer period that brought the family together at different seaside resorts in the north of France, mainly in Normandy[29].

Douglas, Ian and Jeanne, Deauville, 1937

---

[29] See photos in the annex.

Fortunately, Jeanne had her sisters who visited her regularly. Being a small child in France at that period, I have little recollection of those times, except on one occasion when I was left in my cot while Jeanne was in the lounge with some of her sisters. I woke up and I remember standing up and touching something that fell and broke on the floor, thus creating panic next door and bringing everyone to me in great alarm.

I have just two other events that come to mind, a roundabout with small boats at Le Vésinet near the market and I recall a little bell on the boat ringing as we circled. Finally, when we left Paris in September 1938 at the Gare St Lazare on a train to Dieppe, I recall that we said goodbye to my aunts before the train left.

Jeanne adapted herself well to our new life in England and assured our wellbeing at home with good food, a bright, clean and tidy home and much cheerfulness despite difficult moments. We did not have a washing machine, of course, and every Monday morning, Jeanne would literally boil the washing in an enormous galvanised washtub containing a "mushroom" shaped galvanised tube through which the boiling soapy water would come up and spout through the holes in the mushroom head to sprinkle the laundry continuously. Beforehand, the laundry had gone through a sort of pre-wash for the heavily soiled items by Jeanne scrubbing the washing on a corrugated board. Mondays were very tiring for her, but she was always very good tempered. Everything was clean and I would often see Jeanne on her hands and knees polishing the painted floor boards (not nice parquet flooring as we had in France) and I gradually got into the habit of doing my own room and helping her, but she never demanded me to do any chores except occasionally to go the shop to buy some item needed for cooking.

Jeanne, who was not a regular shop goer for women's clothes, did however enter a small fashion shop, called "Elise", situated on Western Road, not far from the Clock Tower in Brighton. In there, she met a wonderful Parisian woman called Raymonde who sowed and adjusted the clothes to the customer's needs, and thereafter commenced a lifelong friendship with our family. Raymonde had married an Englishman called Sydney King who had lived and worked for some years in Paris where they met. Raymonde was full of life, always laughing and joking with a delightful French accent. They had no children. Sydney was very active and did all sorts of jobs, worked hard and did everything to make life good for Raymonde. On some occasions, Nick took Raymonde for a ride on the back of his motorbike and Jeanne stood by in fits of laughter. Some Sundays, with Raymonde and Sydney, we would all go together to the lower promenade on the east side of the Palace Pier now (Brighton Pier) and take a little train going towards Black Rock.

The "Dig for Victory" allotment given to us when we resided at Clifton Terrace, our second requisitioned housing, was a godsend for Jeanne. She was very happy to have vegetables "à volonté" at hand and as a French cook, she always made our meals enjoyable and nourishing. During the war, rationing was in force. We drank less tea than most people and my father often exchanged tea for butter and coffee with his clients. We had margarine of course but Jeanne used it mainly for cooking and for what we put on our bread, we definitely preferred butter! Our breakfast was composed of cold cereals or hot porridge to which we added Golden Syrup and fresh milk, then bacon and eggs, scrambled eggs, or a boiled egg with buttered toast cut into thin slabs for dunking in the yoke, followed by "café au lait" and toast with marmalade or jam. We had brought over from France a hand coffee grinder made of wood with a drawer in which the ground coffee dropped. The coffee beans we bought were of "Continental Roast"!

I had few dislikes with food namely rice pudding that I found too mushy and sweet, and Brussels sprouts at first but I gradually got used to eating them. Jeanne made good omelettes with butter. We ate meat and fish regularly, all well-seasoned and enjoyable. Vegetable soup was the start of the evening meal. Simple mashed potatoes were tasty because well mixed with a little salt, milk and butter. Stale bread was never wasted and ended up with raisins, milk, butter, egg and some grated nutmeg in the oven. The Sunday dining table was well arranged and a pleasure to see and enjoy.

Generally speaking, accommodation in England at that time was not equipped with central heating owing probably to building costs and to the fact that the availability of coal made the use of coal fires popular. Often, there was a fireplace in the front room and other rooms were equipped with gas or electric fire installations used sparingly by putting money in the meter for the required period of use. In winter, bedrooms were only heated a little in advance of going to bed. The cold, bed linen, however, was warmed up by the use of porcelain or rubber hot water bottles placed a little earlier before retiring for the night. These bottles had to be securely closed to avoid catastrophes from water leaks! Jeanne frequently refilled her bottle with freshly heated water when going to bed, as she did not like the cold, and she said that she was about to go to "le Pôle Nord" (The North Pole).

In the morning, Jeanne knelt before the fireplace to collect the cold cinders, the dust of which was very volatile and so she took much care when removing them, but the inevitable film of fine powder deposited on the furniture called for a round of extensive dusting. The next operation consisted of preparing the next fire either for immediate use or for the evening according to the temperature. Old newspaper was twisted and laid down on the hearth, over which pieces of small chopped wood were put before placing fresh coal. When growing up, I would sometimes volunteer to carry out this task. On a very windy occasion, smoke would be thrust down the chimney filling the room with smelly smoke and dust.

Jeanne's spare time was spent sewing, darning socks, utilising a wooden, lemon shaped item in the process of mending holes in socks. She made some of her clothing by knitting and sewing as well as making adjustments to her clothes. Jeanne generally wore navy blue assorted with pale blue blouses or cardigans; sometimes she dressed in black clothes. As she advanced in age she did not put on much extra weight, she kept a good figure, continued to be chic and to walk with dainty steps as a Parisian lady that she was. We had quite a number of French books of our own, plus some supplied by Tante Jeanne and others brought over by Jeanne's sisters after the war and she enjoyed reading classics and popular novels. There was a regular exchange of correspondence between Jeanne and her sisters in France, her writing was a pleasure to see and to read, even in her old age despite the reduced vision of one eye and she fondly drew pictures to illustrate her correspondence. Luckily, a great number of her drawings, many on odd pieces of scrap paper have survived and I have gathered them together in a collection.

We were living in Coldean (on the edge of Brighton) in 1954 when Nick returned from hospital after his last operation and not long after was paralysed from the waist downwards. The house had three bedrooms on the first floor and Jeanne of course had to feed and wash him and it meant going up and down the stairs regularly, but also moving his body that he could no longer control properly. Jeanne was thus exhausted. His condition obviously required proper hospital treatment and he was then sent to hospital for a while. He returned home again, but not long after, he went back to hospital for the last time. Following Nick's death on July 19, 1954, we moved to a smaller two-bedroomed council flat on the first floor at Waverley Crescent situated between Lewes Road and Ditchling Road and much closer to the centre of the town. On the ground floor lived a former Merchant Navy sailor, Francis, and his wife and children who were all very friendly and kind towards Jeanne.

As time marched on, Jeanne had to have her teeth treated, but under the National Health system, teeth were generally yanked out and replaced by dentures with no attempt to reproduce previous appearances. Thus, the new "National Health smile" eliminated the charm of Jeanne's former slight overlap of the top front teeth! Tante

Jeanne also went through a similar treatment and had eleven teeth removed in one go, causing quite an after-shock considering her age!

My military service had terminated on June 27, 1954 and I resumed commuting to London every day as I was working for the Norwich Union Insurance Company in St James' Street next to Piccadilly. In the beginning of 1955, I went to Norwich on an insurance training course at the company headquarters for three months. In that summer, I visited France for the first time since the war. I flew, for the first time in an aeroplane, an "Elizabethan" to land at Le Bourget Airport, near Paris. When this aircraft warmed up its engines it vibrated so much, I felt that it was about to disintegrate! I spent time with my mother's family including my cousin Evelyne at Le Vésinet. The following year, I married Evelyne and we moved to London where she obtained a secretarial job in the City where she could use her French, German and English languages. Thus, Jeanne lived alone for a while, but shortly afterwards her aunt, Tante Jeanne, moved in to live with her. At the end of 1956, I left the Norwich Union and after I worked for a year as an accountant with a Covent Garden trading company. In the summer, I visited Paris looking for a job, but the holiday period was not the right moment for seeking interviews. I then joined the accounting department of the Co-op Travel Service headquarters in London near St James' park. My task was centralising the airline ticket copies sent in by the 52 Coop Travel Agencies for control and onward despatch to IATA for crediting the different airlines the appropriate revenue according to the use of their lines. In September 1958, Evelyne and I decided to sell up and move to Paris permanently. Our first lodging was a small room ("chambre de bonne") on the top floor of the building in Le Vésinet where my aunts Tante Cécile and Tante Madeleine lived.

I started work in November 1958 in a company of British Chartered Accountants auditing customer inventories and nine months later, I answered an advertisement for a position in IBM World Trade European Headquarters situated on the 7th floor of their building at Place Vendôme in the centre of Paris with a staff of 89 people. Evelyme and I moved to the top floor of a house in L'Etang-la-Ville (west of Paris) occupied by a delightful English couple whose children were abroad on their studies. We had a marvellous view overlooking the village in a valley below the other side of which was full of fruit trees that had beautiful blossoms in springtime. Naturally, we kept in touch with my mother Jeanne and my brother, Douglas, and his family by writing and would visit them by taking the train to Dieppe and the boat to Newhaven that was quite close to Brighton.

In 1960, we bought a flat at Louveciennes. In 1964, Evelyne and we divorced by mutual consent and I then resided in Paris.

During a few years Jeanne and her aunt, Tante Jeanne, lived happily together, continuing to take long walks and visiting some of the pleasant Sussex countryside, journeying on the local Southdown buses. Unfortunately, there came the time when Tante Jeanne began to have losses of memory, so much so that when Jeanne retuned from shopping, she would find that the gas stove had been turned on without being lit, as well as other dangerous things which led Jeanne to fall ill with a clot of blood on the brain in 1965. Tante Jeanne had to be placed in a nursing home while Jeanne was successfully operated at Haywards Heath. Jeanne recovered well from the operation and returned home, but she was no longer able to take care of Tante Jeanne who was obliged to remain in a nursing home for the aged

It was when Jeanne was hospitalised in Haywards Heath that I met Odette from Portugal who was on the staff there and we later married on November 20 that year and she came to live with me in Paris. Our first child, Jean-Pierre, was born on September 5 in 1966. We visited Jeanne in 1967 and went to see Tante Jeanne in the nursing home and found that she had bruises on the face. We suspected maltreatment but had no proof and we were told that she had fallen. Tante Jeanne died on October 12, 1967 and was buried on the 16th.

Jeanne had planned to visit her sisters and us in France in the autumn of 1972. Unfortunately, she had a problem with her liver and on September 4, she wrote to say that she had to put off her trip until the following spring. When her health had improved, she did come over in 1973 much to our pleasure. Of course, Jeanne found Paris much changed since pre-war days, and I remember walking happily with her along the boulevard des Capucines and to rue Scribe near the Opéra where she had worked in her early years at the American Express offices. She was pleased to see Paris again, to look at the chic fashions in the boutiques, not yet overrun by chain stores selling ready-made clothes, however she did find that there was too much bustle and hustle compared with the quieter life she now led in Brighton. On my side, I was very happy and proud to show her around the city that I love and knowing that she appreciated this temporary return to her country of origin. Jeanne stayed at her sisters' who lived at Le Vésinet, the town where our family resided before the war and it was another occasion for recalling memories of the past.

Jeanne had to leave her two-bedroom flat at Waverley Crescent and she was allotted a new comfortable single one in a Municipal tower building not far away at Dudeney Lodge on Upper Ditchling Road.

Raymonde and Sydney King, who lived at walking distance away, paid regular visits to Jeanne and Sydney often did some of the heavier shopping for her. During the 1980s, Jeanne fell one night and broke her thighbone and she called for help all night finally to be relieved only in the early morning by one of the attendants of the building. She was operated and then convalesced in a French Protestant Nursing Home near Black Rock.

A second incident of the same kind occurred in the end of 1983. After the operation, Odette went over to stay with Jeanne for about ten days to take good care of her. Jeanne then stayed for while in the Patcham Grange Nursing Home on the edge of Brighton until November 26 following which she was transferred to the Preston Park Nursing Home in Brighton. Douglas who lived in Maidstone was very energetic and went to see Jeanne regularly and took steps to organise her convalescence and to find a long-term solution with a home where she would no longer be living on her own. Finally, in the early part of 1984, she moved into the Loose Valley Nursing Home in the outskirts of Maidstone close by to where Douglas lived. It was a perfect choice; Jeanne was very comfortable there and Douglas and his family were nearby and could visit her easily. It was also ideal for Odette and I who could stay at Douglas's when visiting. She had her own room and was well looked after by the staff. In the grounds of the home lay a very beautiful garden where she could sit out in the fresh air accompanied by the home's Labrador dog that would settle down near her chair.

Although she complained about the failing eyesight of her left eye, at the age of 91, she continued to correspond with her sisters and us regularly and fully in a remarkably clear and well-written style. Although she often said at the end of her letters that writing made her tired, she continued writing and remained completely lucid, and was always concerned with the well-being of her family members. I recall that in April 1987, I visited her and as we were sitting out together on chairs on the lawn, I read to her some French poetry. It has remained an unforgettable and enjoyable moment for both of us.

In October 1987, I accompanied my son, Jean-Pierre, to England for his joining University College to study Archaeology. We stayed at Douglas's home in Maidstone. While staying there, the Loose Valley Nursing Home informed us on October 2 that Jeanne had fallen into a coma. Jean-Pierre went on to London for his registration at the university and Douglas and I went immediately to the nursing home. We relayed each other at Jeanne's bedside and around 2 o'clock in the morning of October 3 when Douglas was with her, she passed away peacefully. She had developed a cancerous tumour of the stomach.

Jeanne was interred in the same tomb[30] as Nick The funeral service took place in the Bear Road Cemetery in Brighton at the tomb-side in the presence of Douglas's family, my wife Odette, Michel and I, Raymonde King and Francis, Jeanne's former neighbour when living at Waverley Crescent. As the presiding pastor did not know Jeanne at all, I read out in French and then in English the homage to Jeanne that I had prepared when travelling to England by boat from Dieppe to Newhaven.

"Jeanne,
Our Mother,
God gave you beauty, charm and a happy and generous nature.
You gave us your love and happiness in our childhood,
You brought us culture and a taste for life?
Jeanne,
Our Mother,
Our Grandmother,
Our Friend,

We have been conquered by your smile,
We have been touched by your kindness,
At all times, we were happy to be with you,
Today we weep, but we shall always keep your smile in our thoughts.
May God reward your goodness and give you everlasting peace."

---

[30] See photo of the tombstone and copy of the homage in French in the annex.

Chapter VII
My Brother Douglas

Douglas – Early days

My parents' second son, Douglas Livingstone was born on December 1, 1925 at the British Hertford Hospital at Levallois-Perret, just outside the west side of Paris.

It must be remembered that his brother, Peter, was three years old then, and he played the part of being Douglas's big brother as they both grew up. The photos showing them together indicate a close relationship. Thus, when Peter died in 1930, Douglas was five years old, and it was a terrible loss for him besides that for Nick and Jeanne. I was born in 1934 and so the difference in age between us was greater, almost eight years and I presume that Douglas must have felt lonely to a certain degree after Peter's death.

Douglas – First Communion at Le Vésinet
(Tante Jeanne, Douglas, Ian and Jeanne)

It appears that it was just before our settling in England that Douglas made his First Communion at the Catholic church of Le Vésinet. A photo shows my mother Jeanne and my great-aunt "Tante Jeanne", both Protestants present at this occasion.

As a result of this difference in age between us (Douglas was eight years older than I), we never spent too much time together and so I was used to being alone with my parents and left to my own devices for occupying my time.

When our family arrived in Brighton to settle down in 1938, Douglas was 13 years old schooled at the Xaverian College, but he had great difficulties in adapting to English as his early schooling in France was in French. Nick had been constantly travelling and I don't imagine that he could have spent much time with Douglas helping him to learn the language.

After arriving in England, it seems that there had been some arguments between Nick and Douglas, but I was too small to be aware of what went on and I was probably kept out of it. Later in life, I learnt about these conflicts between father and son and Nick appears to have been somewhat brutal with my brother, but I do not have any details on that matter not having witnessed any such scenes. It is said that Douglas once went to complain to the police, but I was never told of the outcome. Probably growing adolescence differing with the older generation coupled with aggravation on the part of Nick due to a decline in his health (he was later operated for duodenal ulcer which had caused him considerable pain) may have been the cause for aggravation. Both were certainly affected by the loss of the eldest son, Peter, Nick's first child who was Douglas's elder brother, his play companion. Jeanne loved Douglas very much and was certainly aggrieved by these events. I must say that these events were not a subject that I ever discussed with Jeanne or with Douglas later on. I do, however, recall very clearly the evening in 1954 following Nick's funeral when Douglas and I slept in the same room, he shed tears in his bed. Douglas later often admired Nick's opinion on certain subjects that he talked about, so it seems that love was not lost. Fortunately, through the kind father of one of his schoolmates who understood that Douglas was not happy at school, he got a job at Lloyds Insurance Brokers in London when he was about 15 years old.

World War Service in the Royal Navy

Naval group, Douglas standing 2nd row, 2nd from left facing

At the age of 17, Douglas faked his age and joined the Royal Navy. I was very proud of him. His early missions were devoted to accompanying convoys taking equipment to Soviet Russia after Hitler had attacked the country. He went to Arkhangelsk and to Mourmansk from which he brought back a Soviet red star insignia given to him by a Russian soldier. He was on the HMS Belfast returning from Russia in December 1943, when the German battleship the "Scharnhorst" emerged from one of the northern Norwegian fiords, the "Altenfjord". This occasion led to one of the most important sea battles of the Second World War.

Convoys to Russia discontinued during summer months were resumed in November 1943. In winter months, darkness limited the risk of German military intervention on the convoys by sea and air from their bases in northern Norway. Ice conditions, however, compelled the convoys to pass southwards of Bear Island thus exposing them to enemy attacks. The strategy adopted by the Admiralty to face these threats was to organise the two going and returning convoys to pass each other in this area with their escorts of destroyers and small crafts in good but economic numbers. At the same time, the emergence of the Scharnhorst was anticipated and hoped for as an opportunity to destroy this greatest of the remaining active German battle cruisers that was a constant threat to allied shipping, besides the U boats and air attacks. The 32,000 ton "Scharnhorst", built between 1934 and 1939, had a speed of about 30 knots armed with artillery: 9 x 11 inch (28cm/54.5); 12 x 5.9 inch (15cm/55); 14 x 4.1 inch (10.5cm/65); 16 x 1.5 inch (3.7 cm/83); anti-aircraft guns; 6 x 533 mm Torpedo Tubes.

At this particular time, each convoy had its own armed escorts (destroyers and other craft) but were also accompanied at large by additional fleets organised into two forces: Force 1 comprising of H.M.S. Belfast, on which my brother Douglas served, H.M.S. Norfolk and H.M.S. Sheffield with convoy JW 55A of 19 Merchant ships; Force 2, comprised of H.M.S. Duke of York, Jamaica, Savage, Scorpion, Saumarez, H.Nor.M.S. Stord destined to cover convoy JW 55B of 19 merchant ships. The Isle of Ewe on the northwest coast of Scotland was the assembly point from which Force 1 (Belfast and Co) left for Russia on December 12, 1943, the convoy arriving there safely on December 20. On the same day, Force 2 (Duke of York and Co) left the Isle of Ewe and arrived at the port of Akureyri in northern Iceland on December 21. After a briefing by the Commander-in-Chief, Admiral Sir Bruce Fraser, in preparation for an eventual combat with the Scharnhorst expected to venture out from its hiding place, Force 2 left Akureyri on December 23 at 23h00 sailing towards Bear Island. On December 23 also, Force 1 left Russia at Kola Inlet behind its returning convoy JW 55A (now labelled RA 55A) to pass south of Bear Island, while. In the meantime, the second convoy JW55B that had left the Isle of Ewe on December 20 was about 150 miles northeast of Akureyri and had been located by enemy aircraft on December 23 and was continuously shadowed the next morning. Although the Germans had never ventured westwards for combat, Force 2 speeded to cover the convoy that was situated about 400 miles from

Altenfiord at noon on December 24 because a risk of attack was feared. However, no intervention by the enemy took place.

The next day, Christmas, the returning westbound convoy RA 55A was passing Bear Island undetected so far by the enemy and it was directed to divert northwards clear of the area and to detach four Fleet destroyers (the 36th Division, namely: HMS Musketeer, Matchless, Opportune and Virago) from its escort to reinforce the incoming convoy JW 55B towards Russia, thus bringing the destroyer strength to fourteen. During the night of December 25/26, Force 2 steamed eastwards at 17 knots in an unpleasant sea creating discomfort and a sleepless night. A message received from the Admiralty at 03h39 on December 26 indicated that the Scharnhorst was at sea. She had in fact left Altenfjord with three destroyers at 19h00 the evening before going northwards some 200 miles to the east of Force 2.

The situation at 04h00 on December 26 is shown on the map above with the returning empty Convoy RA 55A having left the area near Bear Island as directed. The incoming convoy JW 55B was now just south of Bear Island with Force 1 going south-westwards to give it cover while the Scharnhorst had already arrived in the area in an undefined position. In the meantime, the Duke of York with Force 2 at quite some distance away at the level of Altenfjord was speeding north eastwards to approach Force 1 with the Belfast under the Command of Voice-Admiral Burnett together with the Sheffield and the Norfolk. At 08h40, the first radar contact was made with the Scharnhorst by the Belfast about 20 miles away whereas the convoy was about 48 miles away further north. The seas were very heavy with strong south westerly winds requiring the regular adjustment of the course and the speed of the ships.

At 09h15, the position of the Scharnhorst as detected by the main radar echo bore 25°, 13,000 yards distance at a speed of about 18 knots. Force 1 formed a line of bearing 180° in the order Belfast, Sheffield, Norfolk, the Belfast being the most northern ship. The line of bearing at 09h21 had just been altered to 160° when the Sheffield sighted the enemy bearing 222°, 13,000 yards. Three minutes later the Belfast fired a star shell to illuminate the scene, and at 09h29 Force 1 was ordered to engage with main armament, the course being altered 40° towards the enemy to 265°. The Norfolk opened fire at a range of 9,800 yards but had to drop back to clear the Belfast range. Firing continued until 09h40, obtaining one hit with the second or third salvo, either on the crow's nest or the bridge port director that caused several casualties with a possible hit on the forecastle. It turned out that Scharnhorst's version of radar in that location was severely damaged and thereby hindered considerably its armed response. The 6-inch guns did not come into action and the enemy did not return fire. Force 1 altered to 105° and then to 170° and the range had increased to 24,000 yards and continued beyond as the Scharnhorst moved at a greater speed, four to six knots more than Force 1 limited to 24 knots. At 09h55, in a mounting snowstorm with difficult visibility, the Scharnhorst altered course to the northeast and Vice-Admiral Burnett understood that she was trying to attain the incoming JW 55B convoy on its way to Russia and therefore he aimed at getting Force 1 in between the Scharnhorst and the convoy. The JW 55B convoy was ordered to turn northwards and to send four of its destroyers to join Force 1 that were then detached at 09h51 to reach Vice-Admiral Burnett on the Belfast at 10h24. Shortly afterwards it was clear that they had lost touch with the enemy.

Shortly after noon, Scharnhorst approached the cruisers again and fire was exchanged. Scharnhorst scored hits on Norfolk, disabling a turret and her radar. On the Scharnhorst, Rear Admiral Bey decided to return southwards to port and directed his destroyers to attack the convoy at a position reported by a U-boat. However, as the position information was out of date, the enemy destroyers missed the convoy. Sheffield and Norfolk dropped back owing to engine trouble as the Belfast, although exposed, continued the pursuit, but she reacquired on her radar set the Scharnhorst whose radar was out of use. At the same time, the Duke of York of Force 2 was pressing ahead from the southwest with her four escorting destroyers to get into torpedo launching positions and having been informed of Belfast's contact, at 16h17 the Duke of York detected the Scharnhorst on its radar at a range of 45,000 yards and then at 29,700 yards fifteen minutes later. At 16h48, the Belfast illuminated the Scharnhorst with star shells making it clearly visible for the Duke of York to open fire at 16h48 a range of 11,920 yards disabling Scharnhorst's foremost turrets and after another salvo destroyed the ship's aeroplane hangar. The Scharnhorst then turned north but the Belfast and Norfolk were bearing down from the north on it, so it then veered towards the east at a high speed of 31 knots to distance these two ships.

It appears that one hit low down on the Scharnhorst caused damage leading to a reduction of its speed. It seemed to lack a clear vision of the exact position of Force 2 and its gunfire became erratic with many near misses of shots at the Duke of York but some of its aerial and radar wires were severed but nevertheless courageously repaired on the mast by Lt H.R.K. Bates of RNVR. At 18h20, the gun duel ceased, the Scharnhorst now moving towards the south. The four "S" class destroyers that had been ordered to attack had made slow progress but were now gaining in their approach as the enemy was slowing down its speed and the destroyers closed in to 12,000 yards and forged ahead. By 18h40, Savage and Saumarez were astern of the enemy while Scorpion and Stord were on its starboard side, the Commander-in-Chief on the Duke of York after seeing the situation on the radar, altered his course and closed in. The Scharnhorst fired heavily but ineffectively at Savage and Saumarez and they returned fire when the range was down to 7,000 yards. During this event, Scorpion and Stord closed in, apparently unseen from the southeast. At 18h49, star shells from Savage illuminated the enemy and Scorpion and Stord immediately swung starboard each firing eight torpedoes at 2,100 and 1,800 yards respectively. Scorpion claimed one hit, Stord none. While retiring, both destroyers were engaged by the Scharnhorst's secondary and light armament, but no damage was sustained whereas they managed to inflict several hits on Scharnhorst's superstructure. The Scharnhorst continued to veer starboard wise to take a south-westerly course, but her movements could be followed clearly in the light of star shells, so Savage and Saumarez on her starboard quarter trained their tubes to starboard to attack at 18h55 despite heavy enemy fire. The Savage fired eight torpedoes at a range of 3,500 yards but the Saumarez due to damage received, fortunately above the waterline, got off only four torpedoes but from a range of 1,800 yards. This action resulted in three significant hits on the enemy: in a boiler room, damage to a shaft and the flooding of several compartments aft, as explained later by some of the few enemy survivors. Savage and Saumarez withdrew northwards at the same time engaging the Scharnhorst that continued on a southerly course at a reduced speed due to the damage.

Coming up from the southwest, the Duke of York and the Jamaica re-engaged at a range of 10,400 yards at 19h01 and scored hits on the Scharnhorst that was still shooting at the retiring destroyers. The Norfolk now joined the battle from the north but had difficulty in finding the right target and then checked fire. When the Scharnhorst five minutes later had been repeatedly hit and fires and flashes from exploding ammunition were flaring up, she shifted her secondary armament on to the Duke of York at a range of 8,000 yards, but fire was intermittent. Between 19h01 and 19h28, the German battle cruiser's speed fell to about 5 knots. At 19h15, the Belfast opened fire at a range of 17,000 yards and then the Commander in Chief ordered it with the Jamaica to close the enemy who was almost stationary, and to sink it with torpedoes. Both cruisers fired to port three torpedoes each with maybe one hit, then they hauled round to fire their remaining torpedoes; the Jamaica at a range of 3,750 yards at 19h37 fired three torpedoes broadside. Prior to that, after the arrival of the 36th division the Musketeer and Matchless from the port side and Opportune and Virago on the starboard side attacked at 19h30. In the meantime, the Belfast who was about to fire her portside torpedoes, considering the number of ships present, decided to leave to go southward to await a better opportunity if necessary. In all, the four Musketeer 36th division destroyers, at ranges between 1,000 to 2,800 yards, fired 15 torpedoes with an estimation of 4 to 5 hits. These torpedoes along with those of the Jamaica were the final blows causing the Scharnhorst to sink accompanied by heavy underwater explosions, between 19h38 and 19h45 difficultly visible due to dense clouds of smoke.

For the next hour, the Belfast, Norfolk and most of the destroyers searched the area for survivors. Little chance was afforded for survival in view of the heavy weather, darkness and icy water. Out of a total crew of 1,968 only 36 survivors were saved, picked up by the Scorpion (30) and the Matchless (6), but no officer was among them.

In conclusion, by ensuring the continuance of the flow of war material supplies to Russia and destroying the last operational German battleship, it was probably one positive way for the allies to satisfy temporarily Stalin's impatience to see his allies opening a second front in Europe for which they were not yet ready at that time.

As for Douglas who served on the Belfast, his role, from what I recall of his account, was to handle munitions to feed the artillery. Due to the dimension of the naval guns, the shells were of an important size and very heavy. His back suffered from this exercise but there was no lasting consequence. He remembered seeing some of the few German survivors who had been saved in the midst of heavy sea conditions, the traditional solidarity between seamen appears to have been fully respected. On the return from an earlier convoy to Russia, Douglas was on the deck chopping up ice covering chains and other equipment, he slipped going over the side but held on a railing desperately not to fall into the cold sea. He managed to get his feet back on deck using the rolling movement of the ship. It was a near thing escaping immediate death.

In 1944, Douglas was stationed near the Isle of Wight where his unit made preparations for D Day. Later, when he came home on leave, I remember that he brought home scrap pieces of the material that was used to make barrage balloons protecting the site against air raids. He also had a few confectioneries that the American forces there distributed generously to their British comrades in arms. He was demobilised in 1945.

Douglas in 1947

Old Xaverians Cricket Club (Douglas in back row facing, 2nd from the right)

In Brighton on August 25, 1955, Douglas married Sheila Crowley (sister of a former Xaverian College pupil with whom Douglas played cricket). He worked in Maidstone in an insurance company, then Manchester and returned to Maidstone where he bought a house at Loose Court. Later, he worked in London, commuting daily mainly by bus coach. He had four children (all successful in their careers), respectively Andrew (Living in Valencia, Spain, married to Mavi; they have a son, Elias), Christopher (single), Juliet (married to Martin and they have a son

Alexander and a daughter Francesca) and Theresa (married to Gavin and they have a daughter Amelia).

My brother, Douglas, and I had never spent much time together in our youth, but as time went by, we began to see more of each other when his family came to France. In the '70s, we had a house in Cabourg, a seaside town in Normandy, and it was great fun when Douglas and Sheila with their children stayed with us. On my side, our family would go to England to visit my mother Jeanne and Douglas's family.

In later years, Douglas liked to play Golf and he began to take me to golf practice when I visited him. Sadly, around 1994, it was found that he had contracted prostate cancer that was diagnosed too late to avoid the spread of metastases. He suffered terribly for several years, at a time when he would normally enjoy retirement. As always, he was most courageous in adversity despite pain and the knowledge of the inevitable outcome.

I spent the Christmas of 1998 at Theresa's home in north London with Douglas and all of his family. Back to Maidstone where he lived, before leaving for France, I said goodbye to Douglas waving from the porch of his house. It was a very difficult moment knowing that he was returning to the care home probably for the last time. In January, we spoke together on the phone, then Douglas died on February 1, 1999, the 4th birthday of his grandson Alexander. Odette, Michel and I attended the funeral and burial at Maidstone on February 10. To me, Douglas was the most courageous of men I have known.

Chapter VIII
Ian (author)

I was born on March 24, 1934 at the British Hertford Hospital at Levallois-Perret on the north-west outskirts of the city of Paris. By coincidence it was on this same day in 1931, that my parents' first child, Peter, died of meningitis. It was only many years later in adolescence that I discovered this fact when perusing the family "Livret de Famille", an official French document given to each married couple for recording the marriage as well as subsequent births and deaths of the family.

I have already described most of my early life in the previously chapters. After the end of my military service and Nick's death in July 1954, I continued to commute to London working as an insurance clerk. For the first time since 1938, I visited Paris in the summer of 1955, staying at my aunts' Cécile and Madeleine living at le Vésinet outside of Paris. I remember taking a Britannia plane to Le Bourget airport. On taking off, the vibrations were so intense that I thought that the plane was about to disintegrate, but it got me there on a rainy day. It was wonderful for me to discover Paris and the outskirts. My aunt Cécile was a good cook and I shall always remember the fine taste of veal of that period (the calves were fed on milk).

In 1956 I lived in Chiswick, London and later I left the insurance company and worked in the accounting company in two companies before deciding to settle in France in 1958 where I started working for British Chartered accountants auditing British subsidiaries in Paris. A year later, I answered an advert for a position in the IBM World Trade European Headquarters in the Place Vendôme, Paris. I worked in the accounts department, then taking on the HQ budget supervising the two sections, then I was transferred to the Western Region Financial section, reviewing country Budget submissions and control. In essence, this period of 8 years was a period of schooling in Finance and General Management by this well-run company with ethics and respect for the staff. This organisation was managed by Jacques Maisonrouge who later joined the management of IBM in the U.S.A. He was much appreciated by all who worked under him and was model of efficiency.

I married Odette in 1965 whom I met in England when she was working in the hospital where Jeanne had been operated at Haywards Heath. Odette has been most courageous with always a pleasant and sweet manner and a perfect mother. We have two sons, Jean-Pierre born in September 1966 and Michel born in October 1968. Odette's Portuguese origins enriched our knowledge and pleasure with her personality, the acquaintance of her country, the people and the culture alongside various holiday resorts that we discovered and enjoyed.

Although I was happy in IBM, promotion was slow, and I had the opportunity of joining the French subsidiary of International Computers Ltd in Paris as Finance Director. After three years, in view of a possible merger with a French computer organisation, I decided to accept similar responsibilities in a French subsidiary of the Canadian Wine and Spirit Company, Seagrams run from New York. After six years and general management changes in 1977, I returned to ICL, but this time at its new European HQ in Puteaux as Regional Financial Controller for Western Europe. In 1981, ICL closed down and at this point, with other colleagues, we formed a computer service company, MG Entreprises, for eleven years until 1992 (the Iraq war encouraged major customers to withhold spending in services and equipment until the future appeared safer). I retired in 1994.

Upon retirement, I studied Chinese at INALCO (the School of Oriental Languages in Paris). Following a Symposium held by several Universities, I translated four articles from French into English for the part INALCO presented by Professor Isabelle Rabut in the publication of "Modern China and the West", edited by Brill in Leiden, Netherlands. In general, I do translations benevolently to help researchers and students as well as some coaching, and social work. Occasionally, I write a bit of poetry for my own amusement.

Jean-Pierre, my eldest son, studied Archaeology at University College in London and is now a Benedictine monk at Flavigny near Dijon. Michel studied at Brighton Polytechnic (now a university) combined with the Polytechnic of Turin, alternatively over four years before getting a Master's in Industrial Environmental Engineering, between Turin and Lausanne Polytechnics to become an Engineer in this field. Michel married Aline and they have a son, Thomas, who is now 20 years old, has passed his baccalaureate exams and is pursuing his studies.

September 11, 2015
At the Abbaye Saint-Joseph de Clairval, at Flavigny in Burgundy
Odette, Thomas, Jean-Pierre (Frère Basile-Marie), and Michel

Chapter IX
My Parents' Brothers and Sisters

Nick's brothers and sisters

Agnes: born on April 1, 1885 at 155 Mordaunt Street, Glasgow. She was a Typist, married John L. Doyle, Engineer's Costing Clerk, on December 18, 1908. The couple later emigrated to the United States of America and I remember them sending us a parcel of food and clothes during the Second World War.

Margaret called "Meg": born April 9, 1886 at 612 Dalmarnock Road. Meg's trace I found in a set of photos she sent to my father in 1916 while he was in convalescence in Scotland and these appeared in Nick's album. They were sent from Switzerland where it seems she was looking after a family's children and had met a couple of English soldiers who were interned by Switzerland as a neutral state in the Great War. Since this discovery, thanks to Sheila and Evelyn's archives (my cousins once removed, daughters of Dorothy, Dolla's daughter), we now know that Meg married her soldier friend Bill and stayed in Switzerland where she gave birth to two girls, Olga and Cécile.

Meg, Olga, Cécile, Bill and a soldier friend

As for **Mary,** born August 19, 1887 at 611 Dalmarnock Road. I knew that she had lived in France because at the end of the 2nd World War, she visited us at Clifton Terrace, Brighton. She mentioned that she had lost a son in the French army resisting the German invasion in 1940. Following my research in Nanterre archives, it is shown that she had married a Dane, **Oswald Kai Buchardt** and lived at 2 rue de Bezons, Nanterre (at that time the department of Seine et Oise). She gave birth, on March 12, 1911, to a girl **Anna Mary** who died on June 7, 1917, no cause of death mentioned on the death certificate. She also gave birth in Nanterre to two sons, **Dominique Guillaume Jacques Pierre** on June 23, 1912, and **Oswald Harold André** on January 8, 1919.

Oswald Harold was later in the French 117th Infantry Regiment facing the invading German troops and killed in action, on June 10, 1940, near Neuilly St Front, (Aisne), "Mort pour la France". He is buried in a Military Cemetery just outside this village, tomb N° 1861[31]. Mary, still residing at N° 2 rue Bezons, Nanterre, died March 23, 1968. Her son **Dominique** died at Clamart (Hauts de Seine) on December 4, 1990. Despite much research in the records after the 2nd World War, **Oswald,** her husband, does not appear anywhere.

Bridget, called "Nettie": born May 12, 1889, at 593 Dalmarnock Road. Profession clerk, married H. K. Anderson from Tennessee USA, a

---

[31] See annex for Oswald's memorial at Nanterrre and military tomb.

widower and a seaman of the United States Navy, on October 29, 1918 at St Peter's Roman Catholic Church in Partick, Glasgow, with her sister Dolla as witness. Presumably, **Bridget** emigrated to the USA.

Peter, Nick's eldest brother was born April 19, 1891 at the same address. In 1914, enlisted in the 1ˢᵗ Battalion of the King's Liverpool Regiment. He was killed in action on November 16, 1914 in Flanders. His name appears with his regiment on the immense War Memorial at Menin Gate at Ypres, Belgium. Nick later dedicated a poem to his memory in his personal album during his convalescence in Edinburgh in 1916.

Elizabeth: born January 8, 1893 at the same address. She appears on the 1911 census and is shown as living at 29 Buchanan Drive with the family of Robert Bird (a muslin manufacturer) as a domestic servant.

Dominick, my father, called "Nick", born April 12, 1895 at the same address.

"Dorothy" called **"Dolla"**: born May 3, 1897 at 115 (Main Street), married **"Gillie"**, Gillaine Donald MacLaine on July 20, 1920 in Edinburgh. **Gillie**, who was born on April 27, 1895, died of TB (tuberculosis) before the Second World War, and "Dolla", then a widow, was living in Brighton with her daughter, **Dorothy**, when our family arrived from France in 1938.

Dolla's daughter, Dorothy, married **Alexander Ogilvie** (at that time a Sergeant in the Royal Air Force) on January 30, 1943 at St Leonard's-in-the-Fields, Church of Scotland, Perth, and subsequently gave birth to two girls, **Evelyn** (born in 1944) and **Sheila** (born in Hove on June 28, 1952).

Dorothy's daughter, Evelyn was born suffering from being deaf and dumb and studied in a specialised school for this handicap and later met Terry Thorne who was in a similar condition and they married on the September 18, 1971 at St Cuthbert's Presbyterian Church, Hove, Sussex. Terry died suddenly of a heart attack on August 25, 2012.

Sheila married **Richard Tillman** in 1972 and gave birth to three children, and she is living in Long Ditton, Surrey. Her first daughter, **Fiona Elizabeth**, was born on August 8, 1974. Her second daughter, **Anna Louise**, was born on August 18, 1981 and married **Anthony** on September 6, 2009 at Downing College, Cambridge. Sheila's third child, a boy, **James Edward**, was born on June 5, 1984 and is at present a student at Chichester, Sussex.

Joseph ("Joe"), born October 4, 1899 at 302 B St Vincent Street, Kelvin, Glasgow. He was last child of Nick's parents, was born on October 4, 1899 at 302 B St Vincent Street, Kelvin, Glasgow. He never married and spent all his life living with his mother **Mary** until she died in 1952. When my brother, **Douglas**, was stationed in the Royal Navy at Greenock in

Scotland during WW2, he visited Joe a few times in Glasgow. Nick, of course, also visited his mother and brother **Joe** after the war.

To summarise, we can see that all the six girls, with the exception of **Elizabeth** whose destiny is unknown, left Scotland; two left for America, one for France, one for England, and one for Switzerland. As for the boys, **Peter** sadly was killed in the Great War, Nick left for France in 1920 and Joe remained with his parents until their death. These family events, emptying Scotland, were not unique at that time.

Jeanne's brothers and sisters

Édouard René, Alfred ("Doudou") born March 23, 1897 at Nanterre was the eldest boy and by his character was much beloved by his family. He studied wood sculpture at the famous Art School in Paris, L'École Boulle[32].

Édouard Gastal à l'École Boulle

---

[32] This history is based on information provided by the INA – "L'Institut National de l'Audiovisuel": After the founding in 1886 of the "École de la rue Reuilly", not far from the Faubourg St Antoine in the historical heart of an area of furniture professionals (cabinet makers, carpenters of various forms of seats, upholsterers, wood carvers), it then became in 1891 "École Boulle" named after the famous cabinetmaker of Louis XIV, André-Charles Boulle (1642–1732). Now modernised and graded as "École Supérieure d'Arts Appliqués", it's a centre of creativity.

When the First World War broke out, he was conscripted into an Infantry Regiment in January 1916. He wrote very regularly to his mother to reassure her, as well as to his sisters and brothers.

When the First World War broke out, he was conscripted into an Infantry Regiment in January 1916. He wrote very regularly to his mother to reassure her, as well as to his sisters and brothers.

Fortunately, a large number of his letters written in pencil on small pieces of paper have been preserved. It is very moving to read the warmth and simplicity of his numerous messages, signed "Doudou", the last letter is dated March 22, 1918 the day before his majority, 21st birthday. He was killed 3 days later on March 25 at Moyencourt, The Somme. He was attributed the mention "Mort pour la France" and the War Cross with the Bronze Star, while it represented a recognition of his sacrifice, it was little comfort for his mother, Juliette, a widow, Édouard's father having passed away in 1917, nor for the rest of his family. Unfortunately, this is just an example, as millions of soldiers and families in France, Great Britain and elsewhere also went through this terrible trauma day by day as the war dragged on. His regular letters to his family show not only the strong ties to his family but also his facility to write well even in the difficult environment of soldiering.

"Doudou" on leave, June 30, 1917

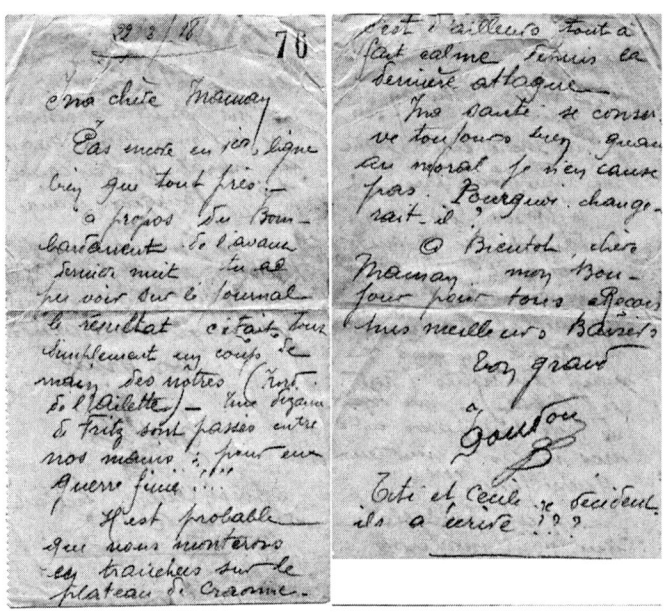

March 22, 1918

Ma chère Maman

Pas encore en 1ère ligne bien que tout près – A propos du bombardement de l'avant dernière nuit tu as pu voir sur le journal le résultat c'était tout simplement un coup de main des nôtres (Nord de l'Ailette) – une dizaine de Fritz sont passées entre nos mains pour eux guerre finie !!!!

Il est probable que nous monterons en tranchées sur le plateau de Craonne. C'est d'ailleurs tout à fait calme depuis la dernière attaque.

Ma santé se conserve toujours bien, quant au moral, je n'en cause pas. Pourquoi changerait-il?

A bientôt chère Maman, mon bonjour pour tous. Reçois mes meilleurs baisers

Ton grand,
Doudou.   Titi et Cécile se décident–ils à écrire ? 22/3/1918

Translation

"*My dear Maman,*

Not yet in the front line although quite near – about the bombardment the night before last you were able to see in the newspaper the result was simply an attack of ours (north of the Ailette River) – ten Fritzs fell into our hands; for them the war is finished!

It is likely that we shall move up in the trenches onto the Craonne plateau. In any case, it is quite calm since the last attack.

My health is still good and as for the morale, I don't talk about it. Why should it change?

Back to you soon, my dear Maman. My greetings to all. Receive my best kisses, your big boy
Doudou   Titi and Cécile have they decided to write?"

Georges, Edgar, born on September 23, 1898 at Nanterre – there is little information to hand about him except that he suffered from the war as a soldier but survived only to die some years later from the effects of his involvement in the conflict.

Jacques, Gabriel, born July 5, 1900 at Nanterre – due to his age, he appears to have been enrolled at the end of the war, conscription still being in force. Later, he married and lived for a time not far from Versailles in Chaville where I visited him in the '60s. He often collected mushrooms in the nearby woods where they were plentiful in the season. He had two children, a boy and a girl. He moved with his wife, Marguerite, to Yvoy le Marron in the department of Loir et Cher where he lived until he was 80/90 years old. He was a very agreeable character.

Cécile, Lucie, Caroline, born October 24, 1901 at Nanterre – she and her sister, Madeleine, with whom she lived for the greater part of her life, worked in the offices of the engineering part of the SNCF (the French Railways). Cécile was much appreciated as a secretary due to the quality of her French as a result of the good cultural upbringing of the family. She corresponded continuously with my mother Jeanne after the war. Cécile and Madeleine went several times to England to see their elder sister, Jeanne whom they revered. She never married and lived until she was 100 years old. I visited her regularly when she was in the old peoples care section of the Le Vésinet Hospital.

Madeleine, Adélia, born December 30, 1906 at Nanterre – she married Auguste Rouvé originally from Alsace, a chemical engineer based in Geneva. Madeleine gave birth to a daughter, **Evelyne**. The couple were eventually divorced, and Evelyne stayed with her mother until the German invasion of France. Evelyne was enabled to take one of the last Red Cross trains going to Geneva to join her father and then went to a boarding school in Basel where she learnt German and finished her schooling. After the war, **Evelyne** returned to France to join her mother who lived with Cécile in Le Vésinet. Madeleine worked also at the SNCF. In 1956

René, born June 28, 1908 at Nanterre – there is not much information at hand on his life. However, I did meet him and his family when he was living in Nantes. He had several children.

Hubert, Louis, born December 28, 1909 at Nanterre – here also there is little information about his life.

Yvonne, born March 12, 1911 at Nanterre – she was very young in spirit and in her company, there was always laughter and amusement. She married a Swiss hairdresser, **Ernest Mürith** and lived in Geneva. They had a daughter **Jeanne Jacqueline** (named after my mother and Tante Jeanne) born July 21, 1942, who presently lives near Geneva. **Jeanne Mürith** worked in the administration offices of a university; she married and has a son, **Philippe,** who has a boy and a girl.

Chapter X
Conclusions

The respect for all those persons that initiated the archives that I inherited, reflecting in their manner of communicating their feelings, conditions of life, experiences, achievements and their messages, is the main reason for writing this book and is why it is my wish to bring these documents to light rather than let them disappear into oblivion.

The history of our families with mixed origins, shows their adaptability and courage when economic and political circumstances provoked uprooting and seeking a new life elsewhere from their native origins. Of course, our families were not alone in these ventures and they have simply been a part of the world's history at particular times. In many ways, material conditions for effecting change may seem easier today for western people, but certainly not for people lacking the means or for those in under-developed countries. Good upbringing and education are factors that count alongside courage and determination in making one's way for the future. Culture is also important and not reserved for an elite and can always be acquired through curiosity and seeking to understand other people and their works; its importance lies in the enrichment of one's mind and a broader understanding of life and of other people.

Without trying to classify the writings in the family archives above their proper place in the ranks of accomplished artists and professionals, my admiration for what I have described and shown arises out of the quality of the written word and the expression of creative ideas for the pleasure of others. Today, it is interesting to observe that at the turn into the 20th century there was no television, no computer systems for the treatment of text, no immediate ways of transmitting messages, but pen and paper, post office mail and telegraph did exist as well as the desire to communicate. The examples presented indicate the efforts made to write well, not only visually but also grammatically, with rarely having to correct what was put on paper. We can also see how sparing the writer was with paper! After having traced the pictures for his story, Jules

Jacques Combe wrote the letter to his daughter Jeanne Jacqueline ("Tante Jeanne") on the reverse side of the drawings!

Tante Jeanne, teaching at Wolverhampton, at the end of June 1914, did a walking tour in Shropshire with a colleague, starting from the Park House Hotel at Shifnal, and she kept daily notes in a tiny 5 x 8 cm black leather bound 68-page notebook about their travels and discoveries. The quality of the graphic writing in this notebook is not as fine as to be found in France at that time, probably because Tante Jeanne's schooling took place in her early days in Uccle, near Brussels with different writing standards, but her observations are interesting.

The content of the letters that survived from the war front written by Edouard Gastal "Doudou", is an indication of the influence Jules Jacques Combe had on his grandson's culture and contacts with his mother and his brothers and sisters. The simple words used are touching, expressed with an attitude of confidence even on the eve of moving up to the front line, and even more so in retrospect knowing now his fate. Not all the millions of soldiers had always the opportunity to write so frequently and undoubtedly, they all had similar feelings and thoughts for the loved ones at home. However, the present testimony underlines the plight of all the combatants in constant danger and estranged from their families.

In Nick's (my father's) album with his characteristic handwriting, he dedicated a poem "Fallen" to his brother Peter killed in November 1914 at Ypres. In my research, I have not found the author and it may well be of Nick's creation. Little matter, it is the gesture that counts, but I mention this to say that poetry was often used at that period as a means of expressing sentiment. Nick also quoted lines from a poem "The Curse of Life" written by Matthew Arnold. Fortunately, poetry is still alive today but a little less in the limelight as of a century ago.

During Nick's career as a textile engineer, constantly travelling from one country to another, he sent a daily report to his Paris office on the customer state of affairs and needs for accessories and replacements, all written on yellow lined paper with blue carbon paper underneath for the copy he retained. It is interesting to observe the difference with today's communication tools. I have noted that, in all the exchanges of correspondence with his office, there is strict formality ("Gentlemen", "Yours faithfully", etc.), but as an engineer, his reports all appear to be meticulously prepared and detailed, and I can understand why the work he accomplished during his career with the Universal Winding Company of Boston was well appreciated by the American Headquarters.

After Nick died and when Douglas and I led our lives elsewhere from Brighton, Jeanne had the company of Tante Jeanne for a while and then she was alone. Fortunately, she had some very good friends in Brighton, and she liked reading and never ceased writing and sketching. She obviously inherited much of her culture from Jules Jacques Combe, her grandfather. After her operation on the thighbone, she could no longer live alone and at the age of 87, she entered a pleasant nursing home close by to my brother, Douglas's home in Kent. Despite a problem with one of her eyes, she still did some reading and continued writing. What I find most remarkable is my mother Jeanne's capacity to communicate by writing so frequently and clearly and attaching her little drawings to her sisters and to my family even at the age of 91 by which time she began to mention the difficulty of her eyesight. These letters are still in my possession but too numerous to add all of them in the annex and so it is for all her sketches. She often added criticisms of her sketches and wrote, "it's not good, but you will find it funny!" She obviously had talent, but she never took herself seriously and always appeared to be in good spirits, a way to overcome difficult moments and times of loneliness. I have added in the annex a card that Jeanne wrote in English to my wife Odette on the occasion of the birth our first son, Jean-Pierre on September 5, 1966. It was well written and very warm in tone. Everything Jeanne did came about naturally and simply. Writing to family and friends regularly is something I have myself inherited to a degree from my mother and I shall be ever grateful to her for that pleasure.

In quoting the War Diaries in the Gallipoli and la Somme war fronts, I should mention that their contents were of course written by hand mostly in the trenches and while bombs and bullets were flying about. The officer making the report had no laptop computer! Communication was much slower having to get a runner to carry back reports and messages to the next level up! I consider these documents to be a most precious record for history.

As for the combatant survivors of the two wars, some were maimed for life or partially handicapped, others sought to live and work again in past or new forms of employment, but what they had experienced was never to be forgotten by them. In all countries, generally state recognition of services was rendered in the form of war pensions after examination and approval, otherwise by medals and anniversaries that may appear trivial but the least that could be done, recognition remaining important. From small villages to large cities in France, and certainly elsewhere, there is an abundance of memorials for the sons who made the supreme sacrifice. Each day of the year (even during the German occupation) at 6.30 pm, the "Eternal Flame" at the tomb of the Unknown Soldier buried beneath the Arc de Triomphe at the top of the Champs Élysées, Paris, is reanimated by different associations and organisations in honour of the fallen soldiers. Since 1931 in France, associations were officially formed to partake in the weekly National Lottery dedicated in part to war invalids such as "Les Gueules Cassées" (The Broken Heads) and "Les Ailes Brisées" (The Broken Wings).

Regarding languages, there is of course a predominance worldwide of the English language in science and world affairs due to historical factors and because it is concise, simpler grammatically and adaptable for making new words. Learning it is not so easy due its irregularities in vocal expression and spelling. The teaching of it abroad often leaves much to be desired. Other languages cannot be ignored because science, culture and creativity exist also outside of the Anglo-Saxon sphere. Today, being bilingual, English and another language, is not enough and it is better to be tri-lingual in which case it is then easier to continue adding another language. It is interesting to note that roughly a third of the English vocabulary has French roots. I consider French to be a beautiful language, notably because it has no tonic accent. Its grammar is very demanding for precision. It is perhaps not preferred for business in so far as expressions tend to be longer, but the vocabulary, well used, is quite precise. I am rather disappointed that youngsters in England seem to shy away from learning French because I often hear that learning Spanish, for example, is easier and that there is a greater world population speaking Spanish than French. That may be so and I have nothing against the Spanish language that is also very beautiful, but I believe it is a mistake not to learn French first because its scientific, technical, intellectual and cultural literature is extremely rich and important, moreover, having learnt French it will facilitate greatly learning most languages of Latin origin. Once you get over the hardest challenge, the rest comes more easily. On the positive side, I have observed that since the creation of various European organisations a larger number of British men and women than before have made efforts to express themselves in excellent French. I'm not sure that the older generation of French people have progressed in English the same way, however the younger French are certainly making efforts in English.

My former history master in college, Brother Aidan, used to say: 'Men learn from history that men never learn from history!' Is that still true? Hopefully, education will let science and technology leave some space for history! Today, after the account I have written describing what men at arms and families endured during and after two worldwide conflicts, my thoughts are now on the challenges that face the younger generations that will have to cope with the present turbulences inside as well as outside our frontiers that we cannot ignore. Within new changing worldwide economic rivalries, they will also have to manage their future with the effect of new technologies, on one hand having to obtain the necessary training to be qualified, and on the other hand, keeping abreast of development. In addition, the climate changes are a worrying reality while threats to peace continue. Many people in the world are in distress and there is a crying need for the maintenance of humanitarian values. A just society calls for fairness of treatment for those of all walks of life. The spread of a new and deadly virus disease leading to a huge loss of lives and economic havoc, will hopefully inspire concrete actions for making Mother Earth a better world for all before it is too late.

Apart from informing the later generations of our family some of its history, I must mention that while the volume of existing souvenirs and documents exhibited here, particularly concerning the wars, may seem excessive, there is a reason. For a vast number of other men and women, active or concerned in one way or another for the defence of their country and who lost their lives, often they probably had little means or the chance to leave such tangible souvenirs after them. Therefore, rather than let the enclosed examples be buried silently, they serve as a witness expressing for all these others unnamed, their similar intimate thoughts, feelings, sufferings, courage and comradeship that existed in those times, that could not be materially recorded.

When ended the two World Wars,
Survivors licked their sores,
Returning to civil life,
They hoped for no more strife.

Efforts for a lasting peace were made,
In Europe for seven decades it paid.
But now, all World events are global,
No longer can we ignore outside trouble.

Some nations seek to impose their might,
In Europe we must better unite,
So that we can defend our rights,
And not be blown out of sight.

Ian MacCabe

Annex
World Wars 1 and 2 – Souvenirs

Gallipoli and Dardanelles Campaign 1915

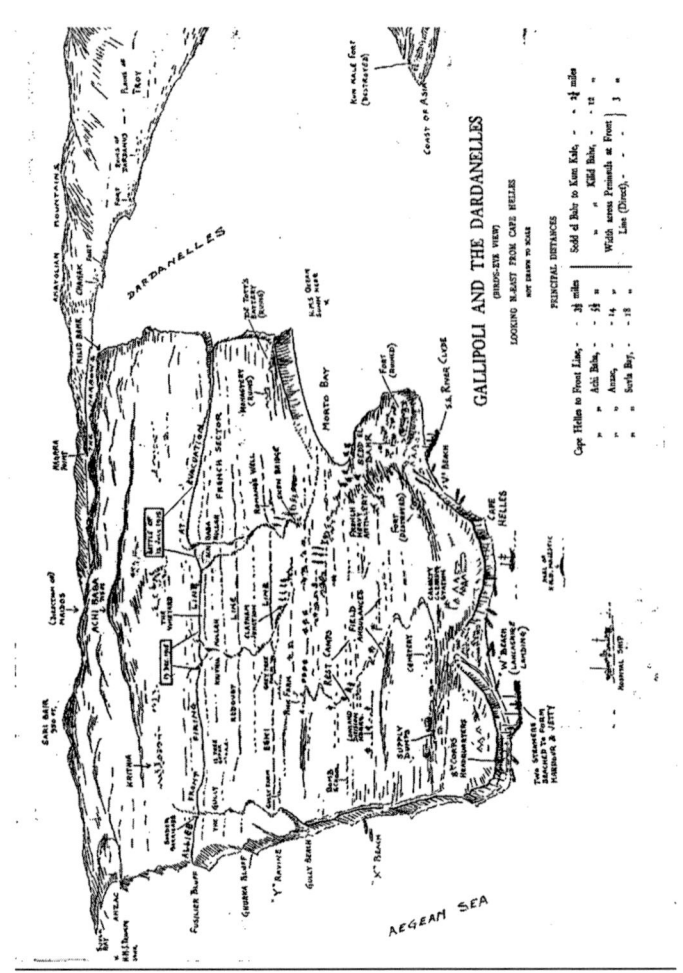

GALLIPOLI AND THE DARDANELLES
(BIRD'S-EYE VIEW)
LOOKING N.EAST FROM CAPE HELLES
NOT DRAWN TO SCALE

PRINCIPAL DISTANCES

Cape Helles to Front Line,	- 2½ miles	Seddel Bahr to Kum Kale,	- 2½ miles
" " Achi Baba,	- 5½ "	" " Kilid Bahr,	- 12 "
" " Anzac,	- 14 "	Width across Peninsula at Front }	3 "
" " Suvla Bay,	- 18 "	Line (Direct),

AEGEAN SEA

Fallen.

Death gained no vaunted victory,
But added only lustre to his name
Who fell and made proud sacrifice
And valour's meet reward - his gain.

And grief by time can be erased,
But fame undying shall remain
To comfort; and the glory of his end
Shall set at naught mere mortal pain.

And what of where he sleeps?
On Gallic soil stained rich and red,
A mould made sacred by his blood;
Fit resting place for honoured dead.

D. McCabe
1916.

Dedicated to my brother.

Dedicated by Nick to his elder brother Peter killed November 16, 1914 at Ypres

When the evening sun is sinking,

And your heart from care is free,

When on absent friends you're thinking,

Will you sometimes think of me?

No 5258,
Pte Wm McCreadie,
2/9th Battn H.L.I.
(Glasgow. Highlanders)

Private W. McCreadie, N° 5258 2/9th Battalion H.L.I. (Glasgow Highlanders)

"Blobs" with Billy Johnson' Dogs. "53 Years, today" Syd Merrills 1916

A wealth of gifts God grants the race of men,
And each gift has its own peculiar price;
Strength, courage, wisdom, love and loveliness,
Yet one the smiles of God supremely bless —
The heroic beauty of Self-sacrifice.

Palgrave.

B B Fuester
Mayfield Red X Hospital

11 March 1916.

B. B. Fuester, Mayfield Red Cross Hospital, March 11, 1916

Dawn.

Low in the East, the first faint star goes out,
Far in the grey beyond the veil of night is torn;
I sometimes think the world is made anew
At hush of dawn.

Deep in my heart the life-love pulses up,
Purer than pearl my longing is re-born;
I sometimes think God bends & kisses us
At hush of dawn.

H Winiver Pauton
Mayfield Red X Hospital

11. 3. 16.

"Dawn", H. Winiver Pauton, Mayfield Red Cross Hospital, March 11, 1916

Never hurry! never worry!
Never fret or fume!
And when the devil shows his face
Just bid him leave the room.

S. Matheson
Mayfield Red + Hospital
April 1916

S. Matheson, Mayfield Red Cross Hospital, April 1916

Just to be a friend of yours
And to know you're one of mine
With a friendship that endures
And grows sweeter like old wine
Just to clasp you by the hand
In a friendly sort of way
And to know you understand
All the things I want to say.

(Not original) The "Colonel"

Mayfield
April 1916.

To my very good friend
Pte. W. McCabe

"The Colonel", (not original), Mayfield, April 1916
"To my very good friend Pte. D. McCabe"

> " And when perchance of all perfection
>   You've seen an end,
>   Your thoughts may turn in my direction
>   To find a friend "

April 1916   A. Reid

           Mayfield Red X Hospital

A. Reid, Mayfield Red Cross Hospital, April 1916

> Just to be a friend of yours
> And to know you're one of mine
> With a friendship that endures
> And grows sweeter like old wine
> Just to clasp you by the hand
> In a friendly sort of way
> And to know you understand
> All the things I want to say.

(Not original.)   The "Colonel"

           Mayfield
           April 1916.

To my very good friend
       Pte. W. McCabe

"The Colonel", (not original), Mayfield, April 1916
"To my very good friend Pte. D. McCabe"

123

There is a saying old and onusty
Yet it is ever true,
Tis never trouble trouble,
Till trouble troubles you.

P. Kinloch
Mayfield Red X Hospital
June 1916

P. Kinloch, Mayfield Red Cross Hospital, June 1916

"And when perchance of all perfection
You've seen an end,
Your thoughts may turn in my direction
To find a friend"

April 1916   A. Reid
Mayfield Red X Hospital

A. Reid, Mayfield Red Cross Hospital, April 1916

There was a young Lady of Lucca, whose lovers completely forsook her; she ran up a tree, and said, "Fiddle-de-dee!" which embarrassed the people of Lucca.

H.J. Hunter, Royal Victoria Hospital, June 30, 1916

Ah, fill the cup :— what boots it to repeat
How time is slipping underneath
                    our feet:

Unborn to-morrow and dead Yesterday,
Why fret about them: if To day
                    be sweet!

Margaret M. Bennet
    Bangour
    —7.16

Margaret M. Bennet, Bangour, July, 1916

"Aunty Nell", Bangour, July 5, 1916

M.H. McGregor, Royal Victoria Hospital, July 28, 1916

Bangour, 4th Sept. 1916.

Lifetime

At ten, a child; at twenty, wild;
    At thirty, wise of never.
At forty, game; at fifty, tame;
    At sixty, rich — or never!

Marg't M. Bennet.

Marg't M. Bennet, Bangour, 4 September, 1916

This is the curse of life! that not
A nobler, calmer train
Of wiser thoughts and feelings blot
Our passions from our brain;

I struggle towards the light; and ye,
O nce longed-for storms of love!
If with the light ye cannot be,
Bear that ye remove.

I struggle towards the light
While yet the night is chill
Upon times barren, stormy flow.
Stay with me, Marguerite, still!

Oct. 5. 1916.

Bangour.

"The Curse of life"
Dominic MacCabe, at Bangour, October 1916

Written By Patients While Convalescing In Whalley, Lancashire, In 1917 On Return From The Somme

Every heart that has beat strong and cheerfully has left a hopeful impulse behind it in the world, and bettered the tradition of mankind.

R. L. S.

M. B. Bell,
Queen Mary's Military Hospital
Whalley. Lancs.

23rd April 1917.

By Robert Louis Stevenson, M.B. Bell, Queen Mary Military Hospital, Whalley, Lancs, April 23, 1917

Loving words will cost but little,
Journeying up the hill of life,
But they make the meek and weary,
Stronger, braver for the strife,
Do you count them only trifles?
What to earth are sun and rain?
Never was a kind word wasted,
Never was one said in vain.

M. Riley
Queen Mary's Military Hospital
Whalley

20/5/17

M. Reiley, Queen Mary Military Hospital, Whalley, Lancs, May 20, 1917.

Love is blind; so we are told —
But this you'll find is true,
That Love on one small chair can find
Sufficient room for two.

———

C. Paton

20/9/17

C. Paton, Queen Mary Military Hospital, Whalley, Lancs, September 20, 1917.

World War I: Convalescence 1915, 1916 in Edinburgh and District. Photos

Nick in his HLI uniform

"Sincerely Yours", Craig

"Sincerely Yours", Syd Merrill and J.W. Robin

Fancy Dress: Patients: Mayfield
Zelen. December 1915.

Group of patients in fancy dress
Zeln at Mayfield — Dec. 1915

December 1915 Fancy Dress party by patients at Mayfield Hospital

Nurses Home Edinburgh War Hospital at Bangour

Interior Recreation Hall Edinburgh War Hospital at Bangour

Service in Ward N° 21 Bangour, 1916

Bangour, January 1916

Mayfield, Edinburgh, March 26, 1916 – Nick laying on right facing

At Royal Victoria Hospital June 1916

Nick, in uniform at Royal Victoria Hospital June 1916

Visit of Edinburgh Zoo July 1916 (Nick on the right facing)

Royal Victoria Hospital, Edinburgh, July 1916

In Whalley, Lancashire,
at St. Mary's Military Hospital, 1917

April 17, 1917 – To Nick, from "Dad"

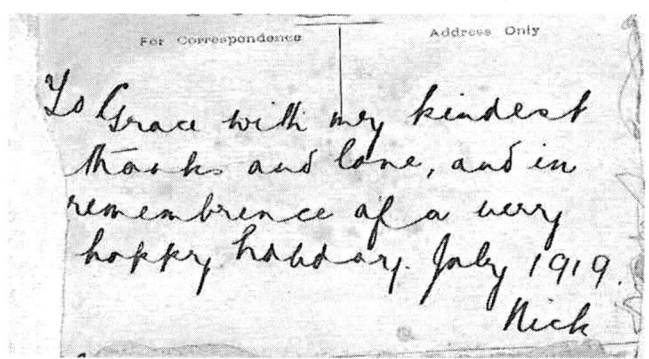

To Grace with my kindest
thanks and love, and in
remembrance of a very
happy holiday. July 1919.
Nick

To Grace, July 1919

The Character here given is based on continuous records of the holder's conduct and employment throughout his military career.

THIS IS TO CERTIFY that No. *41599* Rank *Pte* Name *Domenic McCabe*

has served with the Colours in the HIGHLAND LIGHT INFANTRY for *3* years.

238 days

a sober, honest and diligent soldier.
Discharged on account of ill health Caused
by active service

Signature *Mansbury* Lieut.
for Lieut-Col.
INF. RECORDS.

Date ~~MAR 1918~~ Commanding *Hamilton*

If further particulars as to his character and record of service are required within three years of above date, apply to
where he is registered for civil employment,
afterwards to the Officer in Charge of Records *The Library, Hamilton .*

* This space is intended to be filled in by any organization which has registered the man's name and is prepared to supply further information.

H.L.I.
22210/1064 PARTICULARS OF SERVICE.

Date of Enlistment *12th Aug, 1914.*

~~Proceeded on Furlough pending transfer to the Army~~
~~Reserve, or Discharge on—~~
~~Passed medically fit for the Army Reserve on~~
~~Due for Transfer to the Army Reserve on~~

Due for final Discharge on *6th April, 1918*

Cause of Transfer or Discharge *Being no longer*
physically fit for War Service.
King's Regs. 392. Para. XVI

Campaigns, Medals and Decorations
Home 12-8-14 to 24-5-15
Med Ex Home 25-5-15 to 27-10-15
Home 28-10-15 to 1-1-17
B.E.F. France 2-1-17 to 12-3-17
Home 13-3-17 to 6-4-18

Educational and other Certificates, and dates

D., D. & L., London, E.C.
Agts. W.t.W 8426/2264, 210,000 8/15 Sch. 41.
Form/B. 20671.

Army Form B. 2067.

Serial No. *192*

CHARACTER CERTIFICATE OF No *41599*

Rank *Pte* Name *Domenic McCabe*

HIGHLAND LIGHT INFANTRY Regiment.

Born in the Parish of *Bridgeton*

near the Town of *Glasgow* in the

County of *Lanark* on the

date *12th April, 1895.*

Trade as stated by him on enlistment *Engineer*

* DESCRIPTION ON LEAVING THE COLOURS.

Height *5* ft. *6* in. Identification Marks :—

Complexion *Sallow*

Eyes *Grey* *Nil*

Hair *Dark Brown*

Signature of Soldier *Dominic McCabe*

* To prevent impersonation.

In the event of any doubt arising as to the bona fides of the bearer, the above description and signature should be carefully compared with present appearance and handwriting.

The 1914/15 Star[33], The British War Medal[34] and The Victory Medal[35].

[33] Authorised in 1918, the 1914/15 Star was awarded to those individuals who saw service in France and Flanders from November 23, 1914 to December 31, 1915, and to those individuals who saw service in any other operational theatre from August 5, 1914 to December 31, 1915.

[34] The British War Medal 1914–1920, authorised in 1919, was awarded to eligible service personnel and civilians. Qualification for the award varied slightly according to service. The basic requirement for army personnel and civilians was that they either entered a theatre of war, or rendered approved service overseas between August 5, 1914 and November 11, 1918.

[35] The Victory Medal 1914–1919 was also authorised in 1919 and was awarded to all eligible personnel who served on the establishment of a unit in an operational theatre.

Peter McCabe, Nick's elder brother killed at Ypres Belgium on November 16, 1914. His name figures on the Menin Gate Memorial with the King's Liverpool Regiment:

```
THE KING'S LIVERPOOL REGT.
     PRIVATE                    PRIVATE
LEIGH    T. S.          PICKERING   P.  A.
LEIGHTON   J.           PICKETT   W.  J.
LESTER   J.             PICKFORD  T.  D.C.M
LEWIN   S.              PLANT  A. W. H.
LEWINGDON   A. G.       PLANT   J.  H.
LEWIS   A.              PLEVIN  N.
LEWIS   F. R.           PLUMMER   F.
LIDDLE   S. J.          PORTER   J.  J.
LIDDLE   W.  T.         PORTER   T.  B.
LINEKAR   F.  R.        POSTLETHWAITE  J. A
LISSEMORE   J.  W.      POULSON   A.  H.
LITTLE   A.             POWELL   A.
LITTLE   R.             PRESBURY   H.  G.
LITTLE   S.             PRESTON   J.
LITTLE   T.             PRESTON   R.
LLEWELLYN   E.          PROBERT   T.
LLOYD   H.              PROCTER   W.  S
LLOYD   R.              PROSSER   C.  H
LODGE   J.  W.          PURSLOW . J.
LODGE   W.              PURVIS  R. C.
LOMAS   J.  A.          PYBURN   T. B.
LORD  J.  W.            RAPHAEL   L. B.
LORD  W.                RASCHEN   J.  G
LORIMER  D.             RAWLING  J.  W
LOVATT   J.             RAWLINGS  A.
LOWE  W.  49763         REDDING   J.
LOWE  W.  267476        REDNALL  H. W
LOWE  W.  H.            REES  S. J. L.
LOWENS   J.             REID  D.
LUNN   G.               REYNOLDS   J.
LUNN   J.               RICHARDSON
LYNCH  W.  E.           RICHARDSON
LYNE   S.               RIDDOCH  D.
LYON   T.  H.           RIDING  J.
LYONS   C.              RIGBY  N.  O.
McADAM   J.  C.         RIMMER  G.  I
McATEER   T.            RIMMER  R.
McCABE   P.            ROBERTS   A
McCANN  O.             ROBERTS   G
McCREADY  D            ROBERTS   I
```

Menin Gate Memorial at Ypres, Belgium

Edouard Gastal ("Doudou") – French 279th Infantry Regiment:

At Ursulines Barracks standing 2ⁿᵈ from left with pipe in mouth.

"Doudou, kneeling 2ⁿᵈ on the right facing.,

Letters from "Doudou" in the army in 1916–1917:

To his sister, Cécile, January 24, 1916

Mademoiselle Cécile Pastal.

9. Boulevard de la Seine 9.

Nanterre
(Seine)

Le 27 Février 1917.

Ma chère Cécile

P.S. écris-moi)

Voilà, je t'écris! Es-tu contente?

Merci de tes nouvelles. et je plains amèrement la pauvre jument à Tao de Sable... Enfin espérons qu'elle se guérira!!!!!

Tsoin. Tsoin!! Et tes 2 amies tu ne m'en parles pas. Les 2 miss Willambucher. Te reviennent-elles? Entre parenthèses embrasse-les pour moi - Je vais toujours leur écrire mais je

To his sister, Cécile. February 27, 1917 – page 1

toujours le numéro de l'adresse
si tu y penses. Envoie-le moi
tu seras bien gentille.
Aussi l'orthographe du
nom. Je ne sais pas exactement comment il s'écrit.
— En somme je me porte
excessivement bien. La vie
est ordinairement douce, mais
je pense souvent à mes pau-
vres outils qui meurent s'en-
nui dans leur boîte.
Enfin j'y toucherais peut-
être

Page 2

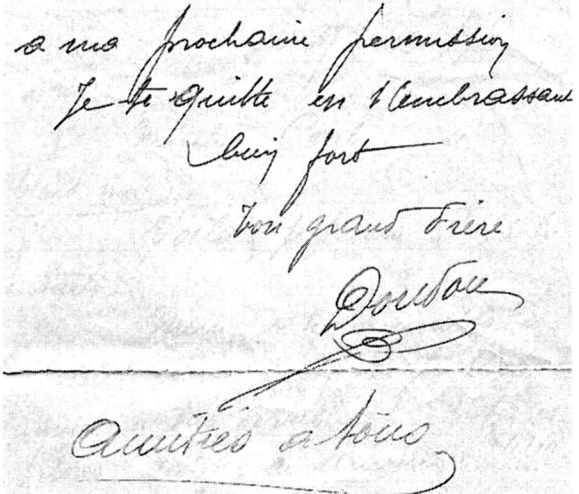

à ma prochaine permission
Je te quitte en t'embrassant
bien fort
ton grand frère

Amitiés à tous

To his sister, Cécile. February 27, 1917 – page 3

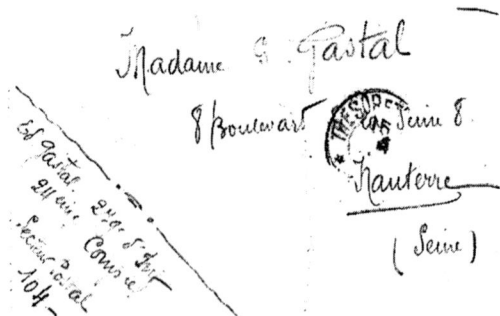

Envelope for letter to his mother, April 14, 1917

Letter to "Doudou's" mother, April 14, 1917

Le 23 Avril 1917

Chère Cécile

Ai bien reçu lettre avec
convocation urgente de l'école
Boulle. C'est un peu tard
et aussi impossible. Je me
demande dans quel but
cette réunion. Demande
a maman si je dois répondre
que je n'ai pu y assister
a cause de ma présence au
front. Pourtant ils doivent le
savoir. Amitiés a tous
Bons Baisers
Doudou

To his sister, Cécile. April 23, 1917

To his sister, Cécile. July 20, 1917

Reverse side of the letter that serves as an envelope when folded.

Le 19 octobre 1917

Ma chère Maman

Un petit mot pour régulariser mes lettres quoique je pense aller à Nanterre d'ici peu. Envoie vivement la dépêche en question pour 2 choses : 1° cela peut faire quelque chose à la santé de Papa et 2° cela me permettra de finir ma période de tranchée à Nanterre ce qui est préférable. Nous pensons être relevés bientôt mais rien n'est encore sûr.

Amitiés à tous et Baisers

Letter to his mother, October 19, 2017

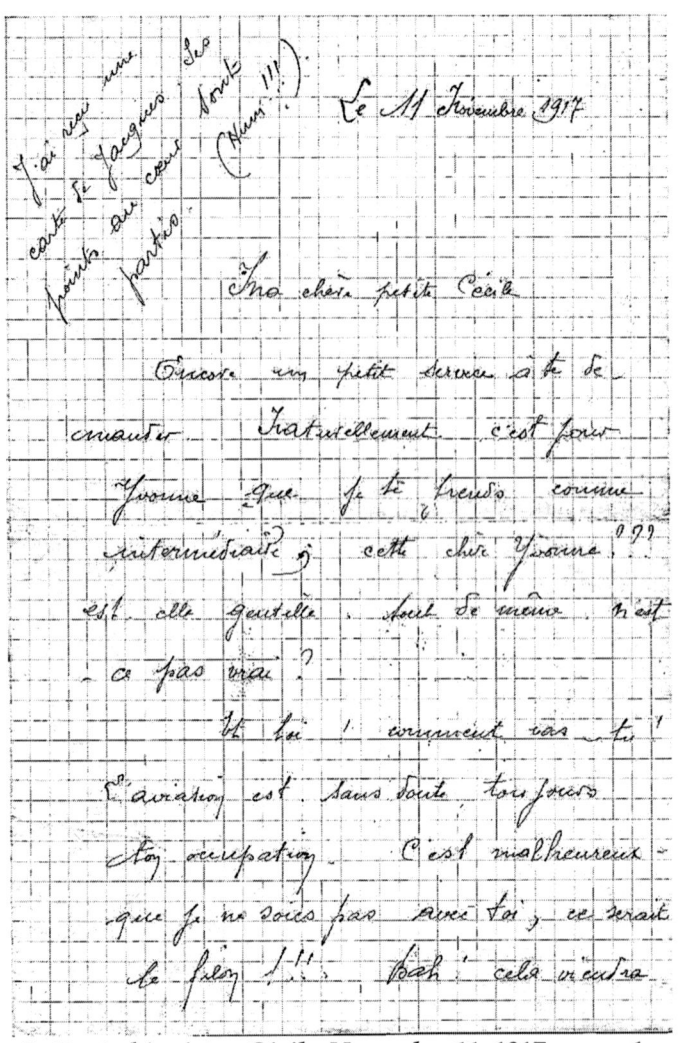

J'ai reçu une
carte de Jacques. Ses
points au cœur sont
partis. (Hum !!!)

Le 11 Novembre 1917

Ma chère petite Cécile

Encore un petit service à te de-
mander. Naturellement c'est pour
Yvonne que je te prends comme
intermédiaire ; cette chère Yvonne ??
est-elle gentille. Tout de même n'est-
ce pas vrai ?

Et toi ! comment vas-tu !
L'aviation est sans doute toujours
ton occupation. C'est malheureux
que je ne sois pas avec toi ; ce serait
le filon !!! Bah ! cela viendra

Letter to his sister, Cécile. November 11, 1917 – page 1

152

peut être il faut pas s'en

faire » comme toujours et

tout le temps « Tsoi Tsoi »

Hein toy grand Tranquin

est bien le même qu'avant il

a toujours la blague à la bou

che c'est ce qui fait le bon

moral du poilu, en satisfaisant

toi même et les copains

J'ai bonne toy bonjour

pour à Edouard, il t'en re

mercie malgré le peu te connais

sance qu'il a de toi Je te

retourne ses bonnes amitiés

J'ai retrouvé tout le

monde en bonne santé, c'est le

Page 2

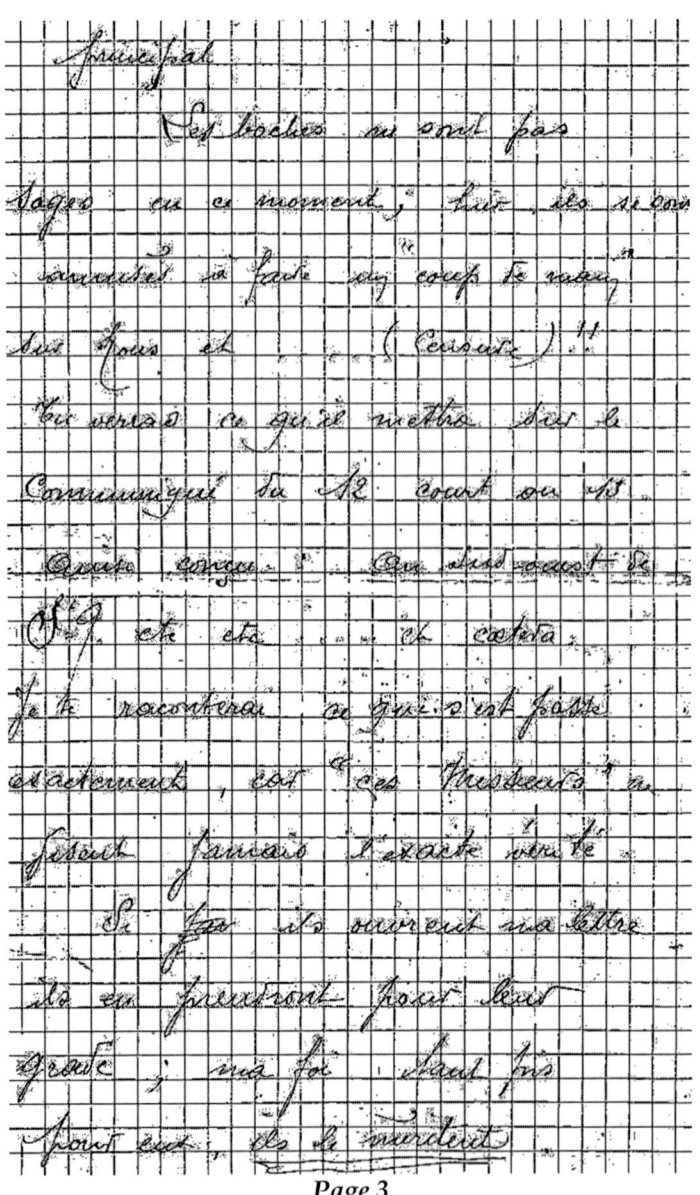

Principal

Les boches ne sont pas
sages en ce moment, hier ils se sont
amusés à faire un coup de main
sur nous et . . . (Censure)
tu verras ce qu'il mettra sur le
Communiqué du 12 court ou 13
Quite comme . . . Au sud ouest de
St . . . etc etc . . . et cætera,
je te raconterai ce qui s'est passé
exactement, car ces Messieurs n'
disent jamais l'exacte vérité
Si ça . . . ils ouvrent ma lettre
ils en prendront pour leur
grade ; ma foi tant pis
pour eux, ils le méritent

Page 3

154

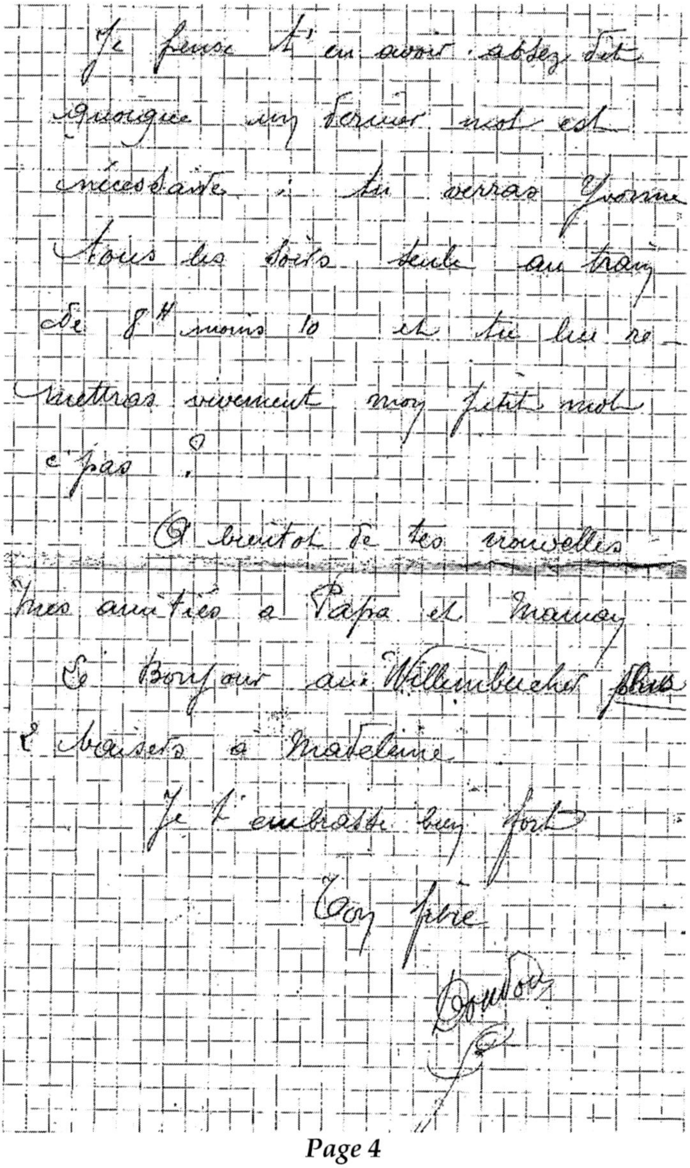

Je pense t'en avoir assez dit quoique un dernier mot est nécessaire : tu verras Yvonne tous les soirs seule au train de 8H moins 10 et tu lui remettras vivement mon petit mot c'pas ?

À bientôt de tes nouvelles

Mes amitiés à Papa et Maman

& Bonjour aux Willembucher plus

& baisers à Madeleine

Je t'embrasse bien fort

Ton père

Boudou

Doudou letter to "Picrati" December 4, 1917 – page 1

("Picrati" is probably Hubert, the youngest brother because he also addresses him as "poussinet" meaning "young chick".)

réveiller !!! Il est 10 H du matin ?

Je passe à la description de mon rêve :

Par un fait que l'on voit que en rêve. Je me trouvais à Nanterre au 2 rue de Bezons. Habillé tout de noir, j'attendais dans l'escalier au 1er étage, ma chère Yvonne ! Elle sortit et nous sommes partis en serrant la main à Mr et Mme Carte.

Tu vois que nous étions bien ensemble !!! Bizarre pas ?

Puis, balade dans notre chère ville pendant quelques temps

Page 2

tout en babillant de choses et
autres ... à un moment donné
nous nous sommes quitté ; elle avait
a rendre une visite ... Encore une
fois attente ....

— Elle revint 10 minutes après et
je lui ai proposé de manger quelques
gateaux chez Prévoux ; elle accep
ta ...! Les gâteaux avalés, nous
voilà repartis et .... réveil
brusque dans mon lit de fer grillagé
— C'était plutôt navrant !
— J'ai oublié un détail qui est
resté net à mon esprit : j'avais

Page 3

158

... mis ses gants, noirs itouta
mais qui étaient grands! c'était
à en mourir de rire.

Tu feras lire ce récit à Yvonne
quand tu pourras, elle va rigoler
tant et plus.

Je souhaite que ce rêve devienne
réalité!!! c'est mon vœux le plus cher.
sauf les gants !!! En attendant je dois me contenter
de manger du "pneu Michelin" assaisonné
de lentilles japonaises extra-dures.
Enfin ... c'est la Guerre!
Terminaison inévitable en cette occasion.
Mes amitiés à Maman et aux enfants
Je t'embrasse bien affectueusement
ton Franguy

P.S. Dis à Jack! que j'ai reçu sa lettre
qu'il n'ait plus de craintes au sujet de l'attaque,
c'est passé et nous sommes même tranquilles.

Page 4

159

Letters from the Front Line in the Somme in 1918

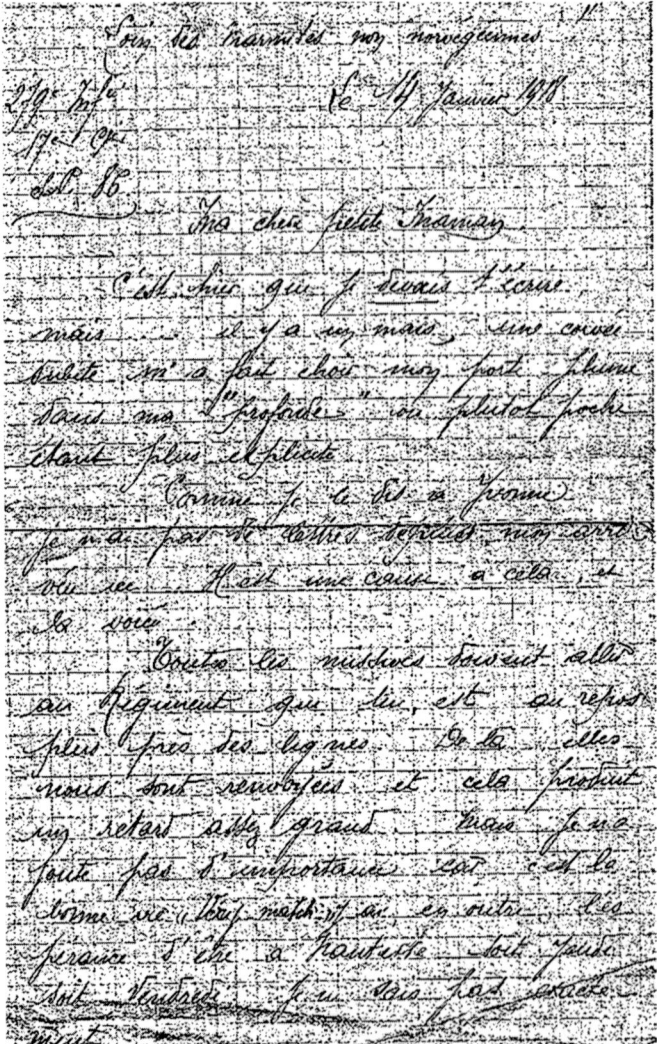

Letter to his mother, January 14, 1918 – page 1

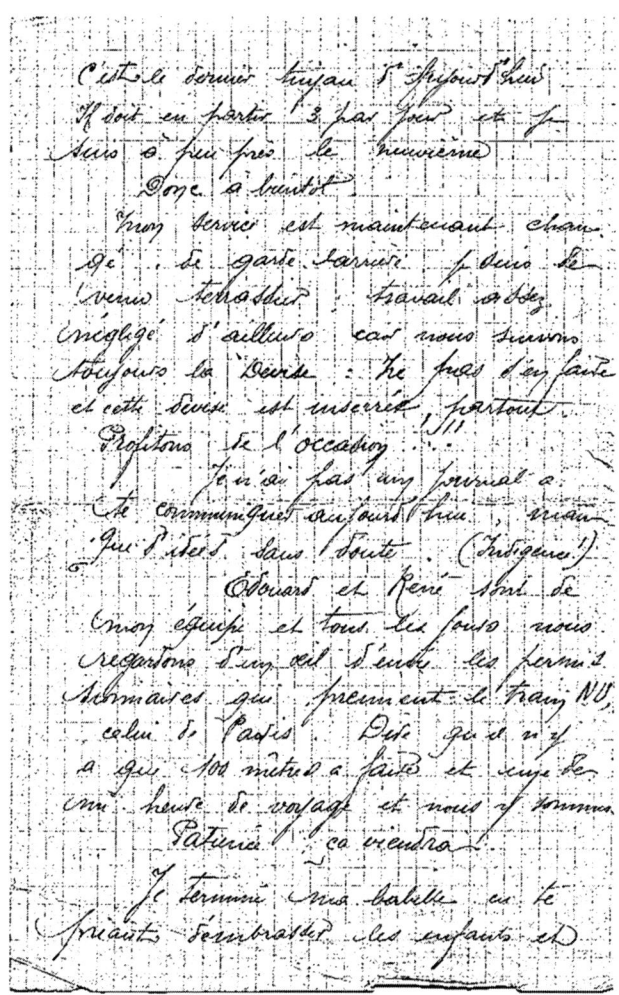

C'est le dernier tuyau d'aujourd'hui
Il doit en partir 3 par jour et j'en
suis à peu près le neuvième
Donc à bientôt

Mon service est maintenant chan-
gé. De garde j'arrive, j'ai du
tenir tchrostier travail assez
négligé d'ailleurs car nous suivons
toujours la Devise : "Ne pas en faire"
et cette devise est inscrite partout...
Profitons de l'occasion !!!

Je n'ai pas un journal à
te communiquer aujourd'hui, rien
que d'idées sans doute. (Indigène !)

Edouard et René sont de
mon équipe et tous les jours nous
regardons d'un œil d'envie les permis-
sionnaires qui prennent le train No.
celui de Paris. Dire qu'il n'y
a que 100 mètres à faire et une de-
mi heure de voyage et nous y sommes
Patience ! ça viendra !

Je termine ma babille en te
priant d'embrasser les enfants et

Page 2

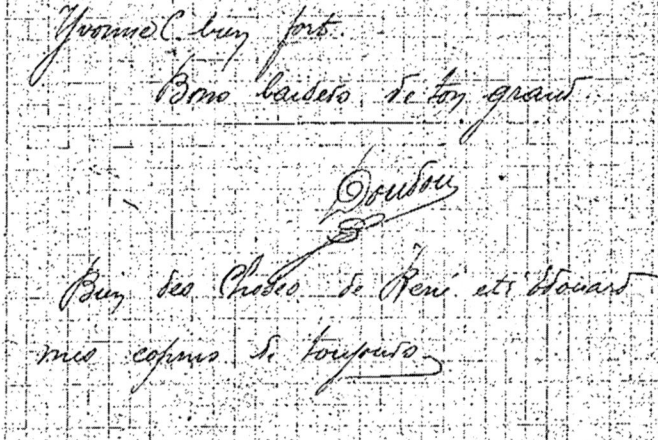

Yvonne C. bien fort.
Bons baisers de ton grand

Doudou

Bien des choses de René et d'Edouard
mes copains de toujours

Page 3

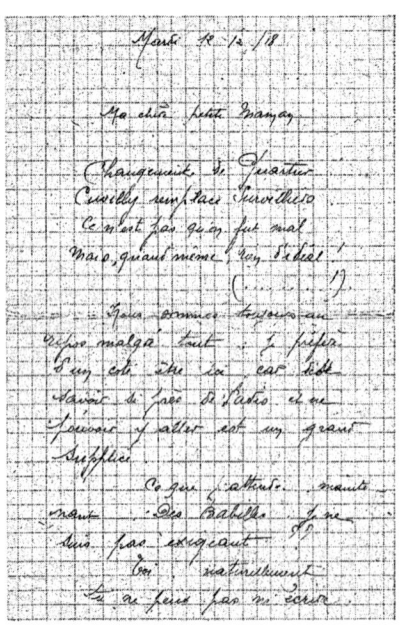

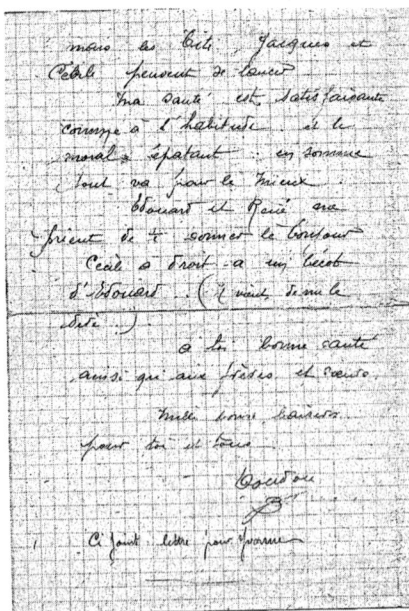

Letter to his mother, February 12, 1918 – pages 1&2

"My dear little Mother,
A change of area Cuvilly to Survilliers. It's not that it was bad but nothing ideal. We are still resting despite everything. On one hand I prefer on one hand being here as knowing not being far from Paris and not being able to go is great torture. What I await now some chatter - I'm not very demanding ... naturally you cannot write to me, but Titi, Jacques and Cécile are thinking of having a go? My health is satisfactory as usual, the morale is good in fact all is well.

Édouard and René say hello to you. Cécile has the right for a kiss from Édouard (he has just said so). Good health to you, as well as the brothers and sisters. A thousand kisses to you and to all. Doudou

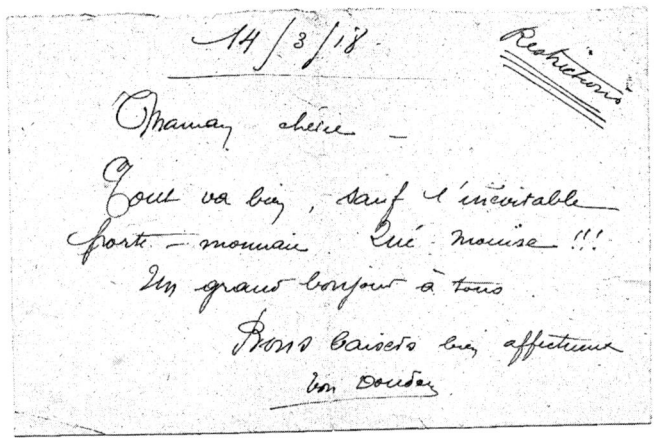

A message to his mother, March 14, 1918

(Note on the top right hand corner. "Restrictions", a security warning.)

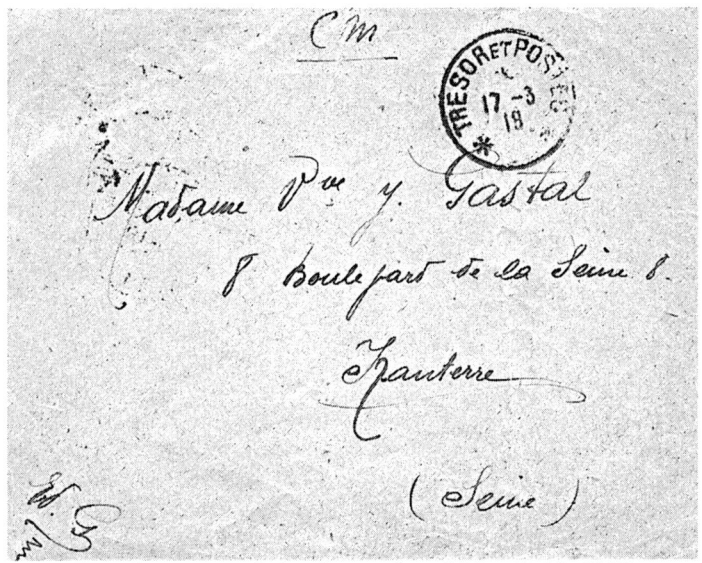

Envelope containing letter dated March 16, 1918

16/3/18

Ma petite Mère chérie

Des tuyaux courent disant notre embarquement pour Lundi. (Destination inconnue) Hum! il me semble entendre déjà la voix des Canons.

Enfin faut pas s'en faire — arrive qui arrive!!

Demain, je vais peut-être à Nanterre, je ne sais pas encore.

Au Revoir chère maman. Mes amitiés à tous

Bons baisers.

Doudou

Letter to his mother dated March 16, 1918

My Darling little Mother, Rumour has it that we are embarking Monday (to an unknown destination). I seem to hear already the voices of the canons. Finally, not to worry, what must be, must be!! Tomorrow perhaps I shall go to Nanterre. I don't know yet. Bye, bye dear Mother, regards to all. Kisses,
" Doudou".

S.G.
2/9 I
17 C
S. 86.

20/3/18

Ma chère maman.

Nous revoici dans la
boue, soi-disant glorieuse.

Pas encore en 1re ligne
mais cela ne tardera pas.

Le secteur, paraît il est
très calme ; aujourd'hui
Fritz profite du Brouillard
pour Bombarder un peu
mais ça ne gaze pas énor-
mément.

Tout va bien, Santé
et Moral. Je conserve toujours ma gaîté en n'importe quelle occasion et je ne
m'en porte pas plus mal
au contraire.
Puis nous reverrons

Letter to his mother dated March 20, 1918

Translation:

My Dear Maman,

Here we are again in the mud, supposedly glorious. Not yet in the front line, but it won't be long. The sector seems very calm; today Fritz takes advantage from the mist to bomb us a bit but there is not much gas.

All is well, health and morale. I maintain my gaiety in any circumstance and I'm not worse off for it, on the contrary.

We are in the area of the "Chemin des Dames", fortunately, it is no longer stormy weather.

A little tired today, so I'll cut short.

Good health to you my dear, little mother, soon for always. Receive from your big boy best kisses.

Greetings to all,

Doudou

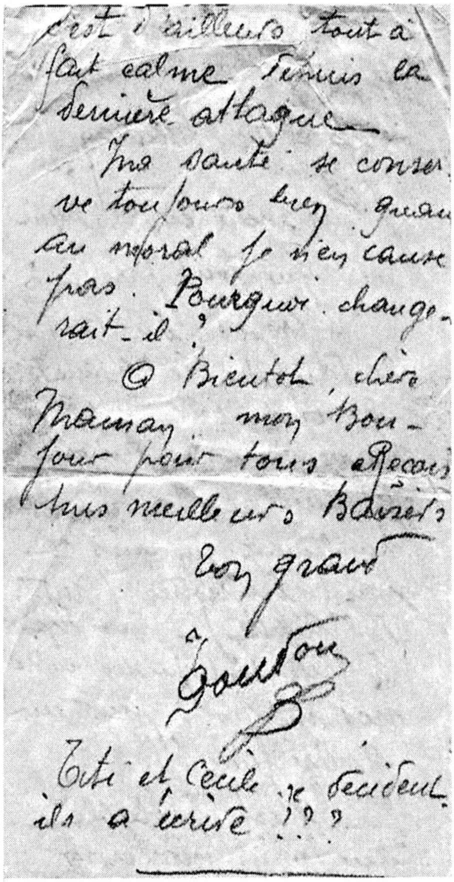

C'est d'ailleurs tout à
fait calme depuis la
dernière attaque.

Ma santé se conser-
ve toujours bien quant
au moral je n'en cause
pas. Pourquoi change-
rait-il ?

@ Bientôt, chère
Maman, mon Bon-
jour pour tous. Reçois
mes meilleurs Baisers

Ton grand

Zouzou

Titi et Cécile se décident-
ils à écrire ???

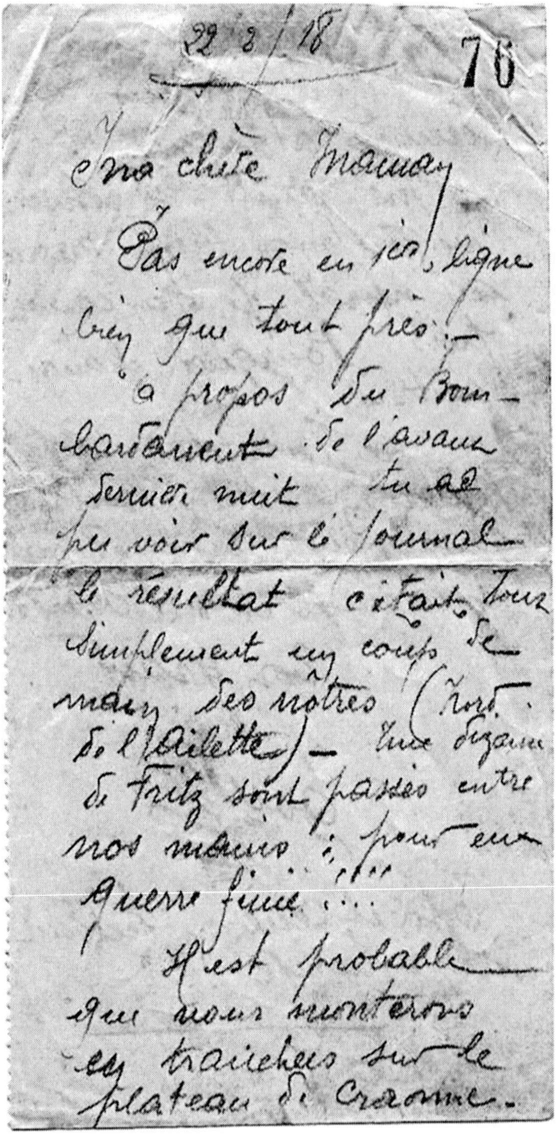

Ma chère Maman

Pas encore en 1ère ligne
bien que tout près ;

À propos du Bom-
bardement de l'avant
dernier nuit tu as
pu voir sur le Journal
le résultat c'était tout
simplement un coup de
main des nôtres (Nord
de l'Ailette) — Une dizaine
de Fritz sont passés entre
nos mains ; pour eux
guerre finie ....

Il est probable
que nous monterons
en tranchées sur le
plateau de Craonne.

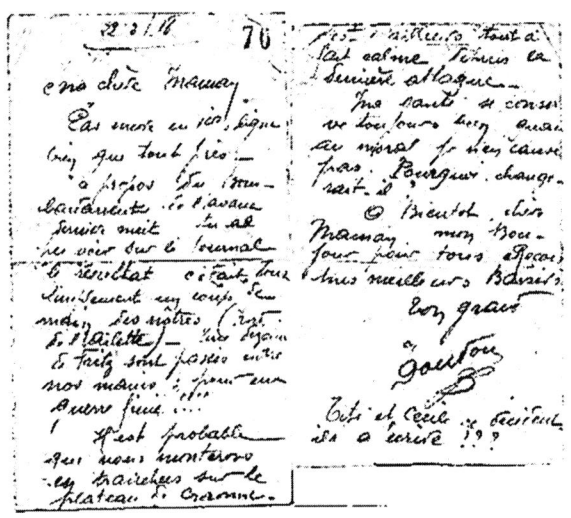

Édouard's last letter to his Mother dated March 22, 1918

Translation :

My Dear Maman,

Not yet in the front line although quite near – About the bombardment the night before last you were able to see in the newspapers the result was simply an attack of ours (north of the Ailette River) – ten Fritz fell into our hands; for them, the war is finished!

It is likely that we shall move up in the trenches onto the Craonne plateau.

In any case, it is quite calm since the last attack.

My health is still good and as for the morale, I don't talk about it. Why should it change?

Back to you soon, my dear Maman.

My greetings to all. Receive my best kisses, your big boy

Doudou

Titi and Cécile have they decided to write?

French original version :

Chère Maman

Pas encore a en 1ère ligne bien que tout près – A propos du bombardement de l'avant dernière nuit tu as pu voir sur le journal le résultat c'était tout simplement un coup de main des nôtres (Nord de l'Ailette) – une dizaine de Fritz sont passées entre nos mains; pour eux guerre finie!

Il est probable que nous monterons en tranchées sur le plateau de Craonne.

C'est d'ailleurs tout à fait calme depuis la dernière attaque.

Ma santé se conserve toujours bien quant au moral je n'en cause pas. Pourquoi changerait-il ?

A bientôt chère Maman, mon bonjour pour tous. Reçois mes meilleurs baisers.

Ton grand
Doudou
Titi et Cécile se décident – ils à écrire ?

Médaille Militaire awarded to Édouard Gastal,
"Mort pour la France"

DUPUIS.F	FRANCAIS	GIBOIN	HANROTE
DURAND.G	FRANCOU	GILLERON	HANROTE
DURAND.M	FRANQUES	GIRARDOT	HARO
DUTERTRE	FRANTZ	GIRAUDOUX	HAUMON
DUTERTRE	FRAPPE	GIROUST	HAUMON
de la COUDRE	FREMERIE	GIVON	HAYE
DUTOIT	FREMIN	GLISIERE	HEBERT
DUVAL.E	FROGER.G	GODARD	HEBERT
DUVAL.L	FROGER.G5	GODEFROY	HELD
ECHARD	FROHN	GOEURY	HENAULT
EMOND	FRONTIER	GONTIER	HENNEQU
ENGRESSAT	FULCRAND	GOREGUES	HENRY
ESCROIGNARD	FUSTER	GOSSENT	HERBET
ESNAULT	GABORIAUX	GOUFFIER	HERY
ETTINGER	GAILLACHE	GOUIN	HESLING
EUSEBE	GALLUS	GOUX	HIDIER
EXCOFFIER	GANDON	GOVET	HOBE
FAHY	GANSTER	GRAILLOT	HODIN
FAILLAT	GARNIER	GRANDIN	HOFFMAN
FARAULT	GASTAL	GRAS	HOFINGER
FASSIER	GATINET	GRENET	HORNEC
FAU	GAULTIER	GRIGNON	HOUDBERT
FAUBET	GAUSS	GRIVIOT	HUBERT
FENAUT	GAUTHERET.A	GRUWE	HUBINET
FERY	GAUTHERET.M	GUERIN	HUBY
FEUILLADE	GAUTHIER	GUILLAUME	HUET
FEYERTAG	GAUTIER.E	GUILLE	HUGEL
FLAMANT	GAUTIER.L	GUILLEMET	HUGUET
FLEURY	GAVE	GUILLERMAIN.A	HUIN
FOISNEAU	GENG	GUILLERMAIN.K	HULIN
FOLTETE	GENTILINI	GUILLORY	HURS
FONTAINE	GEOFFROY	GUYAN	IMBAULT
FOREST	GERBAUT	GUYOT	ISNARD
FOUCALET	GERMAIN.H	HAAS	JACQUEMIN
FOUCAULT	GERMAIN.L	HACH	JANIN
FOUQUART	GESNOUIN	HAMON	JARRY.E
FRACHE	GIBIER	HANNEBIQUE	JARRY.G

1914–1918 War Memorial at the town of Nanterre

MORTS POUR LA FRANCE

1914 ——— 1918

AGENTS DE SERVICE

JAUBERT M. 1914 | SAUTORNIE J. 1916

ANCIENS ÉLÈVES

	PROMOTION		PROMOTION		PROMOTION
LORON L.	1906	DUBOIS A.	1908	LANGROGNET R.	1910
MAURY J.	"	LEFRESNE P.	"	PÉGUET P.	"
OUVRAY H.	"	LEMAIRE P.	"	VIARD M.	"
PONCET R.	"	PROT A.	"	MACHAUX A.	"
RIVET A.	"	ROBERT R.	"	FOREST E.	1911
TIXIER M.	"	RONDELLE P.	"	GASTAL E.	"
BARON L.	1907	SÉNÉQUIER G.	"	KESSLER R.	"
CHAZALETTE M.	"	SIDENNE C.	"	MALÉCOT M.	"
CHEVALEYRIAS L.	"	TÉRIN J.	"	PARADIS R.	"
JÉLIN A.	"	BETAILLE M.	1909	SCHNEEG P.	"
LAURE A.	"	JACOB C.	"	SOURZAC C.	"
LE MAULT E.	"	LEBLANC C.	"	BRUNIER M.	1912
MICHEL R.	"	MARCHOU C.	"	CHÉLIN H.	"
OHLMANN A.	"	MONDON A.	"	DOLLO F.	"
SUQUET E.	"	PEYROUX F.	"	GAUSS F.	"
WARION E.	"	PONCET A.	"	LEBRAUD E.	1913
AGNÈS P.	1908	SIVEL C.	"	GOUVINE H.	1907
AUBRY L.	"	AVERNE A.	1910	RESCHES H.	1912
BATTEAU M.	"	BILLON M.	"	QUIGNARD R.	1904
CHANUT L.	"	BOISSON P.	"		
CHEVAUX C.	"	CHEVILLARD E.	"		
DOUAY R.	"	CIBIER E.	"		

1914–1918 War Memorial at École Boulle

WORLD WAR 2 – Oswald Buchardt (son of Mary MacCabe)

MAIRIE de NANTERRE

Acte de décès
Copie Intégrale

Oswald Buchardt killed June 10, 1940 – Death Certificate

Nanterre 1939–1945 War Memorial

Jules Jacques Combe
- Personal Records

Jules Jacques Combe, Acte d'origine du Canton de Vaud, Commune d'Orbe de 1851

J. J. Combe's French language tutorship for the Grand Duke Inheritor of Saxe Weimar

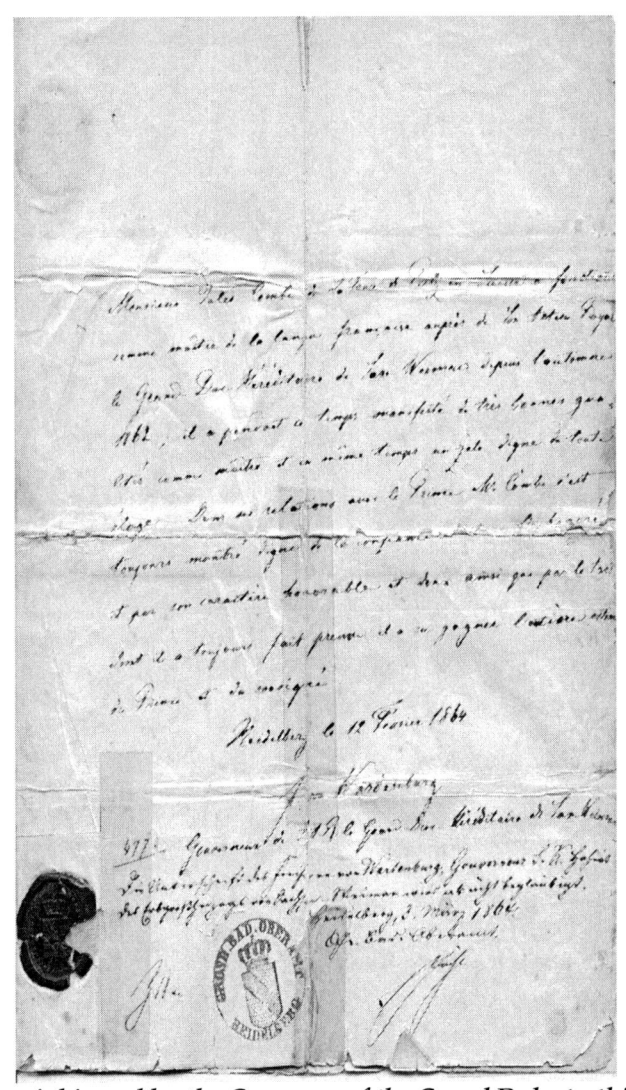

Testimonial issued by the Governor of the Grand Duke to this effect

Ettersburg
près Weimar
ce 4 juillet 1880

Monsieur,

Je viens vous remercier de
votre lettre du 18 juin qui me fit
bien du plaisir, car elle me prouve
que vous ne m'avez pas oublié pendant ces longues années, en partie
si orageuses, qui se sont écoulées
depuis que vous m'avez quitté.

Je ne manque pas de répondre
à votre désir concernant une ré-
férence sur les services que vous
avez bien voulu me rendre; vous
la trouvez dans l'incluse. J'ai cru
pouvoir la faire formuler en allemand,

Letter dated July 4, 1880, in answer to J. J. Combe's request for a recommendation for teaching German – page 1

parce que vous me dites vouloir en-
seigner aussi cette langue. Vous
pouvez en faire l'usage que vous
désirez. Du reste je ne veux pas
omettre de vous informer que nous
n'avons auprès des gouvernements
étrangers aucun représentant spécial;
l'ambassadeur, le ministre ou le
consul allemand est chargé de
veiller sur les intérêts de l'Alle-
magne entière. L'ambassadeur
allemand à Londres est un comte
Münster que j'ai vu à Weimar
il y a bien longtemps.

Les détails que vous me donnez
sur votre personne et votre famille
m'intéressent vivement et je regrette
sincèrement que les rhumatismes vous
forcent d'interrompre votre activité
actuelle. Je me souviens très bien de
vos études en typographie.

Puisque vous ne m'avez pas perdu
de vue, vous saurez que je me suis marié
il y a quelques années et que nous
avons deux enfants. Les hivers nous
les passons à Weimar comme de
raison, dans la bonne saison nous
nous rendons à la campagne et ordinairement à Ettersburg, un petit
château pas loin de la ville. Je
suis heureux de pouvoir vous dire
que moi et les miens nous nous
portons heureusement très bien.
Mr et Mme de Wardenburg sont
sensibles à votre bon souvenir et
me prient de vous faire leurs com-
pliments.

En vous disant adieu je forme les
meilleurs vœux pour l'heureux succès
de votre entreprise.
Avec la considération la plus par-
faite je signe.

Prince August,
duc héréditaire de Saxe

Letter July 4, 1880 pages 2 and 3

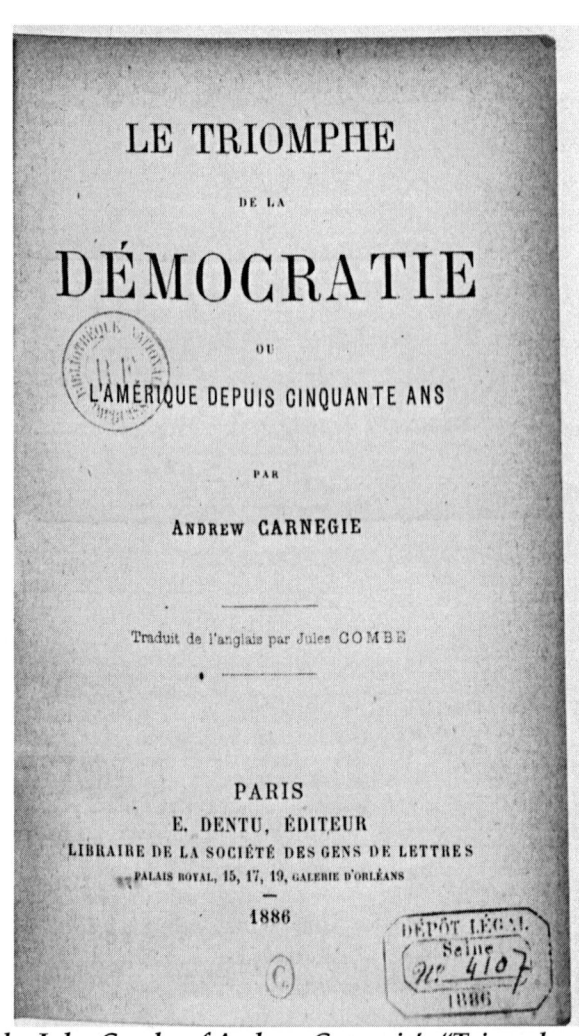

Translation by Jules Combe of Andrew Carnegie's "Triumphant democracy"

Jules Jacques Combe letters to his daughter, Jeanne Jacqueline Combe ("Tante Jeanne")

Jules Jacques Combe to Jeanne Jacqueline
May 25, 1896 – page 1

_2_

May 25, 1896 – page 2

Monsieur Castal, brigadier réserviste
au 22e régiment d'artillerie
1re batterie
France   au camp d'Auvours (Sarthe)

Juliette s'ennuie bien, mais ne le laisse pas trop voir.
Elle va passablement; Fifille va très bien et se civilise
de plus en plus; elle a toujours une provision de
sourires pour moi quand je vais lui faire ma cour.
— Tu me demandes pourquoi j'écris mes lettres avec
une encre et mes enveloppes avec une autre. Cela
tient à ce que je fais mes enveloppes dans mes
moments perdus, pour pouvoir les mouler, puisque
tu aimes ça. Quand je suis au bureau, je les fais
à l'encre noire; à la maison, je les fais à l'encre
violette.
  Je t'envoie sous bande du papier à lettres,
comme tu le demandes.
  Je suis de nouveau pincé par le rhume.
Décidément je n'en sortirai plus.
  Édouard vient de me dire que Louise est
la avec la petite. Je finis ma lettre
...... elle ne partira pas.
  Au revoir ma bonne Louloute.
    Je t'embrasse de cœur
        Ton père affectionné
            J. Combe

Enclosure with the Jules Combe's letter of May 25, 1896 to his daughter, Jeanne Jacqueline Combe.

"The Creation Of The Bicycle"
(translated into English)

Drama written by Jules Combe based on sketches made by Caran d'Ache that Jules Combe traced on the back of this letter, now published here with the kind authorisation of the "Le Figaro" newspaper and also "La Bibliothèque Nationale de France" owners of the sketches.[36]

The actors: The Creator (God)
The Serpent, the Horse, other animals of the Creator
Adam and Eve
The Angel Gabriel, the Coachman
Adam and Eve
The Angel Gabriel, the Coachman

The scene takes place in a garden of earthly paradise.

---

[36] Originated at the "Collection des "Lundis" de Caran d'Ache" published weekly by le Figaro

First Tableau -
The sixth day of the Creation

OR, LE SIXIÈME JOUR, LE BON DIEU S'EST DIT : « JE CROIS QU'IL ME RESTE ENCORE QUELQUE CHOSE À CRÉER... »

The Creator: *I'm beginning to have enough: for six days I haven't stopped; it must be time to have a rest. I created the world, the sun, the moon, stars... Ah! About the stars, why not take one to sit on... There, that's it. Now, let's have a look and recapitulate. I don't think I have forgotten anything: I created the lion, the elephant, the hippopotamus, the giraffe, the dog, the monkey, the cock, the birds, the insects, etc., etc., what can still be missing! Ah!*

By Jove! I was about to make a big mistake: and the bicycles that I was about to forget! That's what it is to get old: we lose our memory! Fortunately, this error can be corrected!

Second Tableau
"Let us have Bicycles!"

ЗА-DESSUS IL S'ÉCRIA : « QUE LES BICYCLETTES SOIENT !»

The Horse: *You then consider me to be nothing! I have all sorts of qualities!*

The Creator: *It's true, we can even do better. I shall create an instrument that will outdistance you in the race.*

The Horse: *What's that?*

The Creator: *The Bicycle. You shall see: Behold the Bicycle!*

Third Tableau
"And Bicycles came about."

ET LES BICYCLETTES FURENT !... LE CRÉATEUR ADMIRA SON OUVRAGE — QUEL
FINI !... QUELS ROULEMENTS !... BILLES PARTOUT !... PÉDALIER ÉTROIT ! ...
« TIENS ! MAIS, SI — SUR CES PÉDALES — JE METTAIS QUELQUE CHOSE ?... »

The Horse: *Oh! Là! Such machines! All I can do is to flee! Let's go!*

The Creator: *Wonderful! These bicycles; what beautiful work! Good, rolling, ball-bearings everywhere! Pedals are narrow! But thinking about it, they are not going to work by themselves; there must be feet to make them move. If I create feet! That's an idea!*

Fourth Tableau
The good Lord created feet.

ET LE BON DIEU CRÉA LES PIEDS!...

Fifth Tableau
"Behold legs, then the thighs, the backside!"

AUX PIEDS, LE GRAND MÉCANICIEN ADAPTA LES JAMBES, AUX JAMBES, LES FÉMURS...
AUX FÉMURS, TOUT CE QU'IL FAUT POUR S'ASSEOIR...

The Creator: *Here we are! It was not as difficult as that! It's wonderful what we can do just by willpower! Simply without much bother, I just said: 'Behold feet!' And that was enough. That is what I say to Evinon, my cook, when she is busy making a white sauce "un roux" (flour and butter) women can be so stubborn!*

But these feet alone don't mean enough; there is a need for legs. While we are at it, we must complete our work.

The Creator: So! What did I tell you regarding willpower? You see them, these legs, these thighs, the backside? Is that sufficiently successful?

(During this monologue, the **Serpent** advanced gently, crawling, then finally climbing on the tree at the foot of which the **Creator** is seated.)

Sixth Tableau
"Let's get a grip!"

A\.or; le serpent survint et souffla à l'oreille du grand Constructeur:
« Mets-y de la variété... pour pouvoir, après, ty reconnaître! »

The Serpent: Oh yes, it's not too bad!
The Creator (jolting suddenly): Hey! Where are you from, dirty beast? Is it permitted to give people such a fright?
The Serpent: Dirty beast! It's easy to say: who, who created me when you think about it? It's not me as far as I know if I crawl, that's your fault; as for me, I would rather walk on two feet like respectful people.

The Creator: Well, you know how it is, my dear serpent, we must fulfil all tastes. If I had only created bi-peds I would never have had enough chairs to seat everyone. I had already created quadrupeds, birds, fish; I had to have reptiles! It fell upon you my dear fellow! You mustn't hold it against me, I shall compensate you, take it easy.

The Serpent (speaking aside): Oh! Yes, you will compensate me, to that I shall reply I am preparing a trick in my way that will make you laugh...less joyfully! (Speaking aloud): Let's speak no more of that. I was saying that it was not so badly done. However, beings that finish with a backside seem to me to be incomplete. They should at least have a torso.

The Creator: That, my goodness, is true! I had not thought of that!

Seventh Tableau
"Behold torsos!"

LE CRÉATEUR ÉCOUTA LE CONSEIL PERFIDE, ET IL MIT DE LA VARIETÉ !
APRÈS QUOI LE BON DIEU CRÉA LES TORSES.

The Creator: *So! What do you say? Is it all right like that?*

The Serpent: *Not bad! Not bad! But who is going to hold the handles of the bicycles? There must at least be hands and arms for these torsos.*

The Creator: *But you are not so stupid, you! So, let's go for hands and arms!*

Eighth Tableau
"Behold hands and arms!"

«ET lE quiDon qui NE SERT à RiEN!...» ViTE il AjouTa lES mAinS ET lES BRAS

The Creator: *You see it doesn't take long: these hands are well adapted to the handlebars; as for the arms, they are well connected to the hands and to the shoulders. I can't see what we can do better.*

The Serpent: *That's not bad effectively; however, if you think that it is finished, you are wrong.*

Ninth Tableau
Bah! What is still missing?

ᴌᴇ ꜱᴇʀᴘᴇɴᴛ ꜱ'ᴇɴ ᴍᴇ̂ʟᴀɴᴛ ᴇɴᴄᴏʀᴇ: «ᴍᴇᴛꜱ ᴅᴏɴᴄ ᴅᴇꜱ ᴛᴇᴛᴇꜱ!...»—«ᴛᴜ ᴄʀᴏɪꜱ?...»

The Creator: *Although I am trying to find out I cannot see what is missing. "Bah! What is still missing?"*

The Serpent: *And what about the heads! Have you ever seen torsos without heads?*

The Creator: *That's quite true, of course! He has some good ideas, this serpent; I can see that we can make something of him.*

The Serpent (speaking aside): *Yes, old man, you can be sure of that; but that something will perhaps not be of your taste...*

Tenth tableau
"Behold the heads!"

«ALLONS, QUE LES TÊTES SOIENT !... » ET LES TÊTES FURENT

The Creator: *Here we are, Serpent, my friend; everything of the best that I can offer.*

Now this time, are you happy? These bicyclists are they of your taste? Now my children get down from your machines and come and salute your creator.

Eleventh Tableau
"Come forward, my children!"

ET ADAM ET EVE FURENT CRÉÉS. «AMUSEZ-VOUS…FAITES DES RECORDS ET AYEZ SOIN DE VOS MACHINES,» DIT LE SEIGNEUR.

The Creator: *First of all, you, what is your name?*

Adam: I am called Adam, p'pa (Dad).

The Creator: *Have you complied with the military laws?*

Adam: Not yet, p'pa; I am only in my twentieth year.

The Creator: *And already married?*

Adam: Yes, p'pa; she's the one that entangled me.

The Creator: *That's your business; I see no problem with that. However, when it will be your turn to be called up, I hope that you will maintain the ancient reputation of bravery of the French army and that you will always march in the paths of honour.*

Adam: Yes, p'pa.

The Creator: *She is, by ma faith, nice, the little one! You are a happy rascal, Adam!*

Adam: Say rather that she is a happy hussy: she makes me go round and round like an uncle.

Eve: Don't listen to him, my little papa: he's a horrible despot, stubborn as a mule. When he wants something, no way can you make him go back… It is true that he only wants whatever I have resolved…

The Creator: *Come on, I see that you are both right. So, my children, enjoy yourselves, break some records, but above all, take good care of your machines.*

Adam and Eve: *Yes, p'pa.*

Twelfth Tableau
"Bad counsel."

HÉLAS !...

The Serpent: *My lovely Eve, your tyre is flat: you could have an accident. I advise you to pump it up before going on the road.*

Eve: *You could be right… Adam! Adam!*

Adam: *What do you want?*

Eve: *Pump up my tyre: The Serpent considers it to be flat…*

Adam: *You are wrong to listen to the advice of the Serpent; I don't trust him; there is something diabolical in his physiognomy.*

Eve: *What does it matter? You're talking rubbish, my friend. Pump up my tyre, I tell you and don't worry about the rest.*

Adam: *Go on, whatever woman would like, the devil wants. Let's do what the devil wants.*

(He fixes the pump and starts pumping. The Serpent shakes with laughter… At the end of a few pumps, the Serpent darts his tongue to the tyre that immediately deflates.)

Eve: *Oh, dear! So, that's done it! We can see that it wasn't a Dunlop! You really needed to pump so forcibly!*

Adam: *I didn't pump hard at all. It's you that allowed yourself to be twisted by that Serpent* **of misfortune! Where is he so that I can settle up with that creature?**

(He looks about for the Serpent who has disappeared.)

The Creator, arriving hotfoot: *Ah! Damn it! What have you done to me here? If that's what you've done with all my recommendations, you are going to get away, and quicker than that!*

Thirteenth Tableau
"Ousted from Paradise."

Adam: Eve, my dear, you have put us in a damn mess: we must get away, and your machine is out of use and mine confiscated.

Eve: dismayed: Unfortunately! My poor Adam, what are we going to do? It's nevertheless by my fault that everything happens to us! If I had listened to you instead of that accursed serpent, we wouldn't be in that state! However, also, why did you give in to me?

(She falls into tears).

Adam: Well, we now have tears! Be consoled, my dear, everything is going to be all right; I have just sent a telegram to Gladiator, the manufacturer of the machines, and they are going to send me two of the most secure models... Look! They're arriving now. Let's mount them quickly and pedal as fast as possible as I perceive papa preceded by a coach and the angel Gabriel mounted on my first machine. They are getting ready to chase us.

The Creator: Oh! They are smart! There they go! My friend Horse! This is the moment for you to show up; I've given you a coach and a coachman; I'm getting into the coach and off you go in pursuit of these fellows. Coachman, a tip of a hundred francs if we catch them; I must know where they stole the machine that they are riding; the angel Gabriel will show us the way.

The Horse: Be reassured my Creator, I know what to do; we shall soon catch them up! Ah! By the way, Coachman, if stings from the whip are part of the game, I'll no longer be in it!

The Coachman: Hey, you weak horse, can't you see that they are increasing their advance!

The Horse: I can't do more than follow Angel Gabriel!

The Creator, putting his head out of the door window: Go on, Angel Gabriel, faster, we are going to lose sight of them!

Angel Gabriel: Ah! Never mind! I cannot go faster! Their machines are going at a hellish speed... I can't understand it; we are much further away from them that at the start!

The Coachman, aiming a telescope on the fugitives: Ah! The devil! Everything is explicable! My friends, it's not worth making greater efforts, we shall not catch them up!

The Creator: *Why then?*

The Coachman: *Heavens! It's very simple: they are riding "Gladiator" machines: I know the make!*

The Horse, collapsing: *Ouf! I am exhausted!*

Angel Gabriel, sponging himself: *I also give up! I cannot go on!*

The Creator: *I must get some of these "Gladiators".*

Adam and Eve looking back at them, thumbed their noses.

(The curtain falls)

Jules Jacques Combe to his daughter Jeanne Jacqueline, July 8, 1906

1

J. COMBE
Ingénieur
Membre de la Société des Ingénieurs civils de France

Traducteur Technique
d'Allemand et d'Anglais

23, Rue du Docteur-Foucault

NANTERRE, le dimanche 8 juillet 1906

Ma bonne jschiote,

Où sont-ils mes beaux jours de Norton, où chaque dimanche m'apportait une longue et intéressante lettre de ma Jeannette, et où moi-même je lui expédiais une lettre non moins longue et aussi intéressante que je pourrais la faire?

Tu avais alors un peu plus de loisirs qu'aujourd'hui et aussi un peu plus de dépendance de ton papa; tu te rendais compte que tu ne vais pas profité de tes années d'école autant que tu l'aurais dû, et à ton âge je me faisais la même réflexion. Moi (d'abord), toi (plus tard) nous avons travaillé pour réparer le temps perdu. J'ai ... des occasions qui m'offraient mes différents moyens d'existence: traducteur, professeur, imprimeur; j'ai eu beaucoup de peine, parce que je n'avais personne pour me guider; mais j'en suis sorti sain de même avec un bagage scientifique et littéraire suffisant pour jeter de la poudre aux yeux de moins instruits, de moins doués et de moins travailleurs que moi. Mon école a duré toute ma vie, et

July 8, 1906 – page 1

aujourd'hui, à soixante-dix ans, j'apprends
encore mainte chose que j'ai résolu de savoir
Toi, tu me ressembles sous ce rapport; tu as
su bien profiter du coup d'épaule que je t'ai
donné, tu as acquis le goût et le besoin de
l'instruction; tu travailleras sans doute autant
que moi, l'exemple de ton père t'ayant appris
qu'il ne faut jamais douter de soi; qu'il faut
au contraire s'imaginer que tout ce que l'on
voit faire par d'autres doit vous être possible.
On parvient ainsi à faire des choses qui d'abord
vous paraissaient matériellement impossibles.
On réussit, dans ces cas-là, mais à condition
de ne pas se laisser décourager par les diffi-
cultés; se reposer de temps en temps, mais revenir à la charge sans tenir de vos échecs
précédents. Le succès final est votre récompense.
Tu as eu un brillant début dans la carrière
d'institutrice, pour laquelle tu sembles avoir
été faite; les demoiselles Daly déjà te rendaient
justice à cet égard en ne tardant pas à te rétri-
buer, quoique tes conditions fussent au pair
avec enseignement de l'anglais. Ces braves
demoiselles ont bien tenu leur engagement.
Puis tes relations avec M. Oger — dues égale-

July 8, 1906 – page 2

197

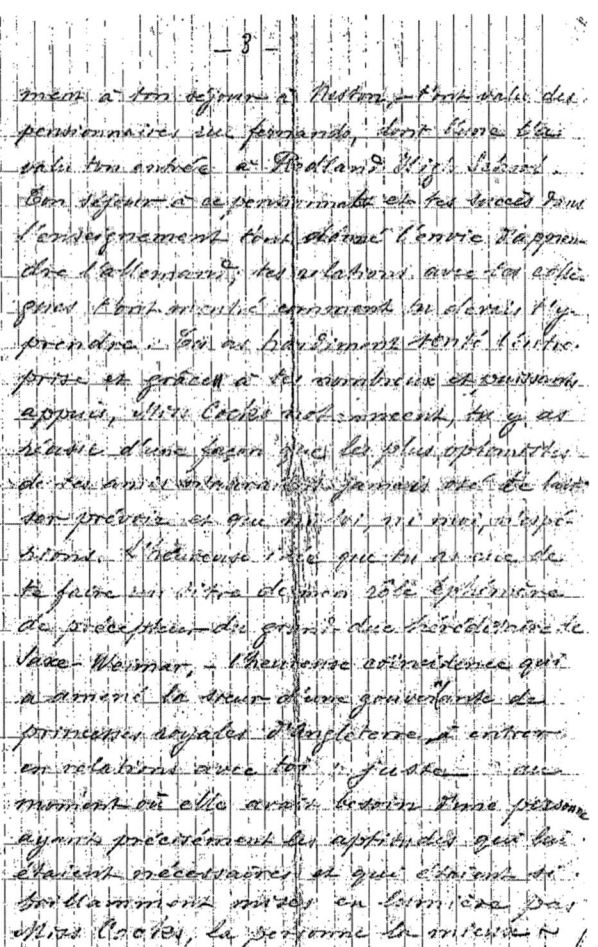

July 8, 1906 – page 3

qualifiée pour le faire, — toutes ces expé-
riences, dis-je, ne sont pas banales, et
quand je me reporte au moment où, il
y a onze ans, je te conduisais pour la
première fois, hors de la maison pater-
nelle, dans un pays dont tu ignorais
la langue, avec un bien maigre bagage
d'études et un protecteur unique, bien
peu influent dans la personne de ton
papa, je dois me dire que, toi et moi, nous
avons été à peu près sans protecteur bien
[...] que mon bien-aimé Louis a vendu notre
cause et en a obtenu le gain.

De tous mes enfants, tu es la seule qui
ait si bien réussi, sous tous les rapports,
dans une période aussi prolongée, et je
bénis l'auteur de toutes choses qui m'a
accordé cette joie pour mes vieux jours,
en compensation de la douleur terrible
où m'aurait plongé la mort de mon
bien-aimé.

N'oublie point ces choses, ma fille, et

July 8, 1906 – page 4

dans tes pensées sur ce sujet, dont, depuis
qu'elle existe, la créature humaine cherche
vainement à pénétrer le mystère, sois
reconnaissante envers l'auteur de toutes
choses, qui t'a si visiblement protégée,
et qui m'a protégé moi-même depuis
ma plus tendre enfance jusqu'à ce jour.

Je reviendrai sur ce sujet un autre
jour. Pour aujourd'hui, je me borne
à cet avant-propos, dont je ne conserve
pas copie; c'est pourquoi conserve ma
lettre.

Didier a reçu ta carte et me l'a
lue. Je ne l'ai pas sous les yeux et
je ne me rappelle pas s'il y a quelque
question qui demande une réponse.
Je ne le crois pas; dans le cas contraire
je t'enverrais une carte postale.

Pour terminer un peu gaiement,
je t'envoie deux boutades sorties récemment de ma forge.

Voici d'abord la conclusion d'un
discours de ce personnage fameux,
créé par Henri Monnier; je veux

July 8, 1906 – page 5

dire M. Prudhomme, qui pour remercier ses électeurs qui lui avaient voté
un sabre d'honneur, s'écrie, les lar-
mes aux yeux:

« Mes amis... ce sabre... est le plus
beau jour de ma vie !!! »

Voici la somfe bien enthousiasbé,
que j'ai imaginée d'un discours que
je suppose avoir été prononcé par l'illustre
Prudhomme; _if there is but one_
« ...et s'il n'y en a qu'un, dans
le monde entier et dans les colonies,
pour faire son devoir, je serai
ce qu'un-là !!! » (Tonnerre d'applau-
dissements.) _I shall be this_ « but-one »

Autre boutade: Maxime à l'usage
de tous et de tous les jours:

« Quand on veut se mêler d'être
malhonnête, il faut être du métier;
sinon on ne fait rien de bien. »

Traduis-moi cette maxime en anglais
correct: ce doit être facile et ça amusera
ton monde. Je t'embrasse de cœur.

Papa

July 8, 1906 – page 6

Jules Jacques Combe to Jeanne Jacqueline, January 13, 1907

January 13, 1907 – page 1

pris de mon humble personne pendant les jours de fête m'ayant amené à vomir à plusieurs reprises, je me suis senti tout d'un coup beaucoup mieux, d'où j'ai conclu que ce que j'avais eu n'était autre chose qu'un embarras gastrique; maintenant j'ai de nouveau bon appétit et le point au cœur m'a quitté. tout est donc pour le mieux. — Mais une autre raison tendrait également à te faire interpréter le ton actuel de mes lettres dans un sens défavorable à ma santé et je tiens à te mettre en garde à ce sujet. le ton n'est plus aussi familier que lorsque tu étais à Bristol ou à Weston: d'abord tu étais plus jeune... et moi aussi; mais le milieu n'était plus le même et mes lettres pouvaient tomber dans danger pour toi entre des mains étrangères: les sujets parfois un peu enfantins et délicats qui y étaient traités étaient de nature trop française pour pouvoir être interprétés dans un sens qui, jugé au point de vue anglais aurait pu t'être défavorable. Ils n'auraient pas été compris, et par conséquent mal interprétés. Mais il n'en est plus de même dans ton milieu actuel; tu n'es plus une enfant et la situation m'oblige à une retenue égale à celle que j'aurais si, étant près de toi, je devais te parler en français devant des personnes d'un monde fort distingué, comprenant le français aussi bien que l'allemand. Là, le ton paternel familier n'est plus de raison. Or il faut que je prévoie le cas où l'une quelconque de mes lettres pourrait s'égarer et tomber sous les yeux de personnes à qui elles pourraient paraître étranges, de la part d'un père de 70 ans, adressée à une fille de 30. Je sais bien que, dans le milieu fort bien élevé où tu te trouves, une telle éventualité n'est pas à redouter: la discrétion la plus sévère y fait partie des règles du bon ton. Mais de toute façon, j'estime qu'il arrive un moment où un père, quelque habitué qu'il soit à la plus tendre familiarité

January 13, 1907 – page 2

January 13, 1907 – page 3

On this page, Jules Jacques explains a French grammatical point regarding the use of the accusative or dative form of the object, direct or indirect between the verbs *"suivre" (follow),* or *"succéde*r *(succeed).*

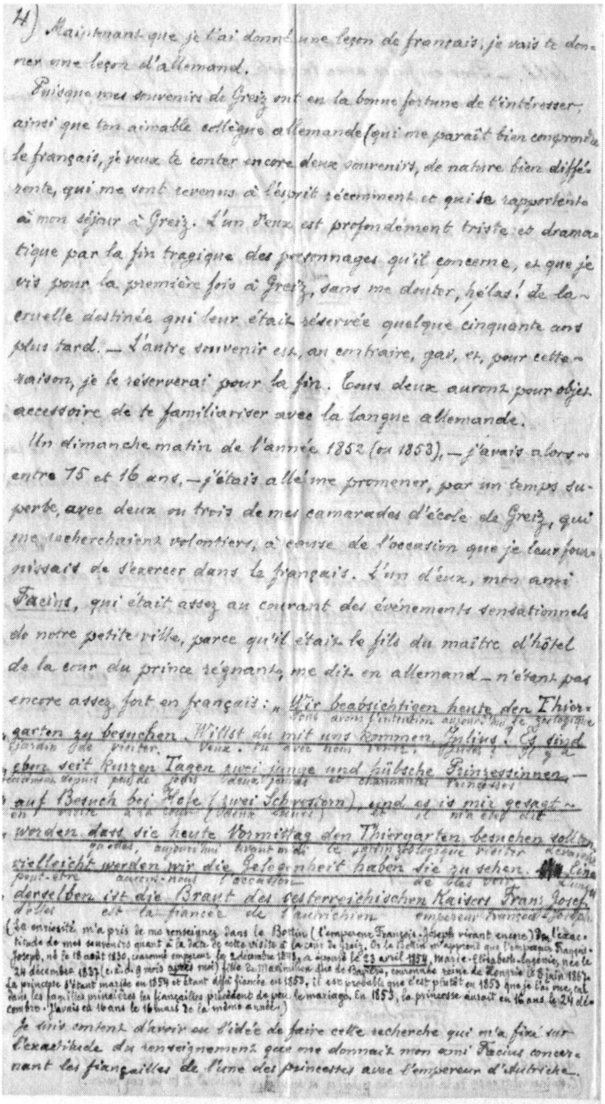

4) Maintenant que je t'ai donné une leçon de français, je vais te donner une leçon d'allemand.

Puisque mes souvenirs de Greiz ont eu la bonne fortune de t'intéresser, ainsi que ton aimable collègue allemande (qui me paraît bien comprendre le français), je veux te conter encore deux souvenirs, de nature bien différente, qui me sont revenus à l'esprit récemment et qui se rapportent à mon séjour à Greiz. L'un d'eux est profondément triste et dramatique par la fin tragique des personnages qu'il concerne, et que je vis pour la première fois à Greiz, sans me douter, hélas! de la cruelle destinée qui leur était réservée quelque cinquante ans plus tard. — L'autre souvenir est, au contraire, gai, et, pour cette raison, je le réserverai pour la fin. Tous deux auront pour objet accessoire de te familiariser avec la langue allemande.

Un dimanche matin de l'année 1852 (ou 1853), — j'avais alors entre 15 et 16 ans, — j'étais allé me promener, par un temps superbe, avec deux ou trois de mes camarades d'école de Greiz, qui me recherchaient volontiers, à cause de l'occasion que je leur fournissais de s'exercer dans le français. L'un d'eux, mon ami Facius, qui était assez au courant des événements sensationnels de notre petite ville, parce qu'il était le fils du maître d'hôtel de la cour du prince régnant, me dit en allemand — n'étant pas encore assez fort en français: „Wir beabsichtigen heute den Thiergarten zu besuchen. Willst du mit uns kommen, Julius? Es sind eben seit kurzen Tagen zwei junge und hübsche Prinzessinnen auf Besuch bei Hofe (zwei Schwestern), und es is mir gesagt worden dass sie heute Vormittag den Thiergarten besuchen sollen, vielleicht werden wir die Gelegenheit haben sie zu sehen. Eine derselben ist die Braut des oesterreichischen Kaisers Franz Josef."

(La curiosité m'a pris de me renseigner dans le Bottin (l'empereur François-Joseph vivant encore) de l'exactitude de mes souvenirs quant à la date de cette visite à la cour de Greiz. Or le Bottin m'apprend que l'empereur François-Joseph, né le 18 août 1830, couronné empereur le 2 décembre 1848, a épousé le 23 avril 1854, Marie-Elisabeth-Eugénie, née le 24 décembre 1837 (c.à.d. 9 mois après moi) fille de Maximilien duc de Bavière, couronnée reine de Hongrie le 8 juin 1867. La princesse s'étant mariée en 1854 et étant déjà fiancée en 1853, il est probable que c'est plutôt en 1853 que je l'ai vue, car dans les familles princières les fiançailles précèdent de peu le mariage. En 1853, la princesse aurait eu 16 ans le 24 décembre. J'avais eu 16 ans le 16 mars de la même année.)

Je suis content d'avoir eu l'idée de faire cette recherche qui m'a fixé sur l'exactitude du renseignement que me donnait mon ami Facius concernant les fiançailles de l'une des princesses avec l'empereur d'Autriche.

January 13, 1907 – page 4

[Here, Jules Jacques treats a question on German grammar and translation as well as a historical event.]

Jules Jacques Combe to Jeanne Jacqueline, January 27, 1907

January 27, 1907 – page 1

« ...et bien que son allemand fût médiocre !... »

Ah ! pour le coup, c'est trop fort ! après m'avoir dit qu'elle trouvait mon allemand admirable !!!

« J'aurais pu tout de même apprendre quelque chose si elle -
« m'avait parlé allemand... »

Je comprends, je comprends : Jeanne voudrait que j'écrive tout en allemand ; elle se contenterait de cette médiocrité ! Faute de grives on prend des merles ! Elle n'y va pas par quatre chemins ! Mais il me semble qu'elle aurait pu me le dire tout de suite, sans user de ces circonlocutions blessantes. Continuons :

« ...mais non, elle aimait trop parler français, avec un accent
« formidable !!!... »

Ma correspondance !... un accent formidable !!! Ah ça ! est-ce que Jeanne deviendrait folle ?...

« ...et une voix !... ce n'était pas une trompette, mais un vrai trombone !

(Mes cheveux se hérissent sur ma tête ! Ma correspondance une voix... une trompette... un vrai trombone !!! Plus de doute ! la musique de Wagner lui a tourné la cervelle ! Il faut que, sans tarder, je télégraphie à Fräulein Nödel pour la prier de faire examiner Jeanne par un aliéniste !...)

Heureusement que l'idée m'est venue de regarder au bas de la page² où je lis ces quelques mots qui m'expliquent tout :

« Mon Allemande qui appréciait tant
page³ ta correspondance est partie, et, entre nous, je n'en suis pas fâché.

Tu peux te représenter si je me suis tordu dans le train en faisant ces réflexions. Il y avait deux dames qui me regardaient en souriant. L'une disait à l'autre : « Ah ! mais regar-
« dez donc ce jeune homme, comme il est gai ! » L'autre lui répondait : « Oui, c'est un âge heureux, où l'on voit tout en
« rose, mais soyez tranquille, ça se passera : on ne rit pas
« toujours dans la vie !... »

En voilà une vieille grincheuse, cette femme ! je l'ai bien regardée ; je suis sûr qu'elle avait bien trente ans, si ce n'est plus. Ces vieilles-là, ça ne comprend pas la jeunesse !

January 27, 1907 – page 2

207

J'ai trouvé ta petite sœur fraîche comme un bouton de rose et jolie comme un cœur. Ça lui va de faire la nounou; comme ton excellente mère, elle ne se porte jamais mieux que durant ses grossesses et son nourrissage. Elle n'a jamais eu de masque, tandis que ta mère en a eu un — je ne me rappelle pas à laquelle de ses grossesses — et elle l'a toujours conservé. — Juliette me charge de te dire que ta petite Madeleine te ressemble encore plus que les autres: quant à moi, je ne me prononce pas à cet égard: je ne crois pas que l'on puisse, chez un bébé de cet âge, affirmer une ressemblance quelconque. Dimanche dernier, ou sous un certain jour, il m'avait paru avoir une vague ressemblance avec petit Jacques; aujourd'hui je n'ai rien vu de pareil. Quoi qu'il en soit, c'est ce que l'on peut appeler un beau bébé, très bien portant et s'entendant fort bien avec sa maman. Durant la demi-heure que j'ai passée près d'eux, je ne les ai pas entendus se quereller une seule fois. Tu me diras peut-être que ce n'est qu'une demi-heure et que la journée en comprend 48. Qu'importe! c'est toujours ça de trouvé; si je devais être tourmenté pendant 47 demi-heures, je ne serais pas fâché d'avoir la quarante-huitième pour prendre un peu de repos.

Juliette compte rentrer chez elle dimanche prochain. — Georges a heureusement beaucoup de travail: voilà plusieurs dimanches qu'il va passer l'après-midi à ton bureau, et tous les jours il fait des heures en plus. Comme d'habitude, il y avait un tas de monde chez Cartier: dame! rien que les enfants des deux ménages, cela fait dix, et avec les papas et mamans quatorze.

Didier me charge de te dire qu'il n'a pas encore pu se procurer la liste du dernier tirage de ta ville de Paris; il sait par les journaux que ton obligation n'est pas sortie, et il aurait pu t'envoyer la découpure du journal où il l'a vu; mais il voulait t'envoyer la liste officielle, mais il a laissé passer le jour où on la vendait dans les rues; il ne l'a pas entendu crier le lendemain; il en a acheté une quelques jours plus tard, mais elle ne contenait pas ce tirage: il s'était fait tromper par un de ces crieurs qui lui a repassé une vieille liste ou une plus récente, mais ce n'était pas celle qu'il lui fallait. Il va faire en sorte de se la procurer au bureau qui les publie et il te l'enverra aussitôt: il ne sait pas où est ce bureau, mais il va s'en informer.

Ça m'ennuie de t'envoyer une page blanche: il me semble que la poste ne m'en donne pas pour la valeur de mon timbre. Mais il se fait tard et il faut que je me lève à cinq heures. Je n'ai rien reçu de toi cette semaine; j'en conclus que tu travailles ou que tu t'amuses ferme et je ne t'en parle que pour la bonne règle. J'ai tenu à aller ce soir chez Juliette pour le cas où lui aurais écrit en joignant quelques mots pour moi; mais elle n'a rien reçu non plus. Nous t'embrassons tous de cœur.

Ton père affectionné J. Combe

January 27, 1907 – page 3

(a) Juliette Gastal to her sister "Tante Jeanne", July 15, 1928

1920 – 1938 FAMILY LETTER

Grand centre
élevage Gastal

Bertrancourt le 15
Juillet 28

adresse Mme Gastal
chez Mr Carlier fils
à Bertrancourt par Acheux
Somme

Ma chère petite soeur

Je suis ici depuis Vendredi, le
voyage n'a pourtant pas été très
long 3 heures de Paris à Albert
néanmoins j'étais bien fatiguée
et mes jambes fléchissaient
sous moi, Cité m'attendait à
la gare, nous avons pris ensuite
un petit train que l'on nomme
un tortillard parce qu'il serpen-
te à travers la plaine, il ne
faut pas être pressé, c'est une
véritable brouette. Enfin us
sommes arrivés tout de même
mais je n'en pouvais plus.

From Bertrancourt, July 28, 1928 – page 1

209

Tante Madeleine m'attendait
et je me suis un peu récon-
fortée avec une tasse de thé
et des biscuits après quoi ns
sommes allés dans la maison
de Geogeo et de nono qu'ils
partagent en ce moment
avec Gaby en attendant
une autre. J'ai été très
surprise au sujet de Ber-
trancourt, je ne croyais
pas que c'était si gentil
L'air y est très pur et
je crois que je vais reprendre des forces. On me soi-
gne faut voir ça. Le
matin après ma toilette

From Bertrancourt, July 28, 1928 – page 2

Gogo m'installe dans le
jardin sur une chaise
longue et je me sens
si bien là que j'y reste
jusqu'au déjeuner de midi
Mon appétit semble vouloir
revenir petit à petit et j'ai
parait il un peu de couleurs
chose qui m'avait quitté
depuis longtemps.

Je vais manger du poulet
rôti et des petits pois du
jardin et un appétissant
gâteau que Nono à confec-
tionné ce matin.

Ma mignonne sœur je

From Bertrancourt, July 18, 1928 – page 3

vait tâcher de reprendre le
dessus j'en ai bien besoin.
Geoges et Tino voudraient me
garder un mois, mais le
puis-je? Et ma bande
là-bas et toi ma petite
sœur qui doit bientôt
venir. Enfin nous verrons
comment je serai au bout
de deux semaines.

Je n'ai pas pu écrire
plus tôt car avec ces
jours de fête la poste ne
marchait pas.

Merci beaucoup ma
chérie pr les 2 lignes que
tu as eu la bonté de m'envoyer
Bons baisers
Juliette

Tino et Geoges t'embrassent bien

1920 – 1938 Family Photos

Juliet Gastal, Tante Jeanne, Papa, Maman, Peter, 1923

Peter at Nanterre, 1923

Tante Jeanne – August 1923

Peter with Papa Nick at Plestin les Grèves July 1925

Douglas and Peter, Nanterre 1928

Jeanne, visitor, Douglas and Peter,
Nanterre September 1928

Douglas and Peter at Ste Honorine – August 1929

Ste Honorine – August 1929

Douglas and Papa Ste Honorine 1931

Papa (smoking) and Ian Deauville 1937

Papa (smoking) and Ian Deauville 1937

Ian at Deauville 1937

Papa, Ian and Douglas Deauville 1937

Papa, Ian and Douglas Deauville 1937

Douglas carrying Ian, Deauville 1937

Maman, Ian and Douglas, Deauville 1937

Ian, Deauville, 1937

Douglas, Ian & Papa, Deauville, 1937

1920–1939: Business Photos and Correspondence

Germany

Eastern Europe

Eastern Europe

Leipziger Hasa – Germany 1931 (Nick with beret)

Germany 1931

Germany 1931 (Nick on left facing)

Bosphorous view from Asian side, Turkey, June 1934

Galata Port, Turkey, June 1934

*With customer Leggeris & family, Vouliangmeni,
south of Athens, August 15, 1934*

Nick's Exchanges with Universal Winding Co of Boston (U.W.C.) – Paris and Boston offices

Nick in Holland to UWC Paris
January 4/5, 1938 – page 1

D. MacCabe.

Hotel de Graaff, Enschede

15 Feb. 38.

Re letter Luggeris concerning Chaboche price list.

Gentlemen, It will be best to cover yourselves by obtaining a C.I.F. price le pièce and communicate same to Luggeris who will himself give you word about definitely ordering and paying in the way he suggests, or by deduction on commission outstanding to him. Re mastic: It will be necessary to enquire from Chaboche how much of this is required to re-line the stove in question, and the cost should figure on the quotation. You are right in supposing the parts should be shipped "no charge", as replace of damaged ditto.

Luggeris would like you to definitely order and pay for these and that they should be shipped C.I.F. le pièce, but in view of the financial control in Greece I see the your hesitation to undertake this and that is why I suggest you submit the quotation to him before taking any further action.

I am, Gentlemen Yours faithfully

D. MacCabe ____.

Nick in Holland to UWC Paris February 9, 1938

J. MacCabe.

Leiden, Holland

14 Feb '38

J.T. Cars to braf Ruge Work, Hengelo.

Gentlemen: herewith please find the Collation Report Repr Sheet of R.O.I. # covering the erection of the #10 #C at above concern.

The m.c is giving entire satisfaction, and its work should ensure the acquisition of other similar units. Yarn being wound are dyed sewing cottons up to 11,100 yards per cone, the Tester Root Counters are very favourably regarded here and are an improvement on any other so far seen by Mr. Reitsmalla.

The fitting charges: In order to settle the question of actual time spent in erecting and adjusting this m/c I suggested 3½ days and so & the same, collected his money and the railfares Paris – Helmond return.   3½ Days @ 15 Gal. Q.t.: 52.50
        Retn Paris Roosendaal (3846 6) 21.84
         + R'daal Helmond   12.90
"all received and credited in my ex book 47.24
Clients will confirm this o.t need.

Hope you agree I did best to collect this, as all discussion is avoided in what was an annoying situation — and 3½ largely covers the actual work. I am going to Paris with tomorrow and will only report on the situation there, and then proceed to Gouda.

I am, Gentlemen, faithfully yours
        J. MacCabe

Nick in Holland to UWC Paris February 14, 1938

Gentlemen,

You will recall that I informed you verbally last September that owing to family reasons I would be obliged to return to England. At the same time I made known to you my desire to remain attached to the Paris office of the Company, and to continue my work under your direction.

The question of your retaining my services was, at that time, referred to the head office, and since then I have received no word from you concerning any decision arrived at. I now beg to inform you that the reasons already mentioned oblige me, to my great regret, to leave France with my family at the end of next March.

In view of this departure, and in the event of your being unable to keep me in your employ while domiciled in England, I shall, to my profound regret, and bound by the duties to my family, be definitely leaving the Company's service at the end of March next.

I am, Gentlemen,

faithfully yours

J. MacCabe

Nick in Greece to UWC January 14, 1938

UNIVERSAL WINDING COMPANY

SIÈGE SOCIAL BOSTON. E.U.A

R.C. SÈRIE N°101.931

LEESONA
MARQUE DÉPOSÉE

TEL. BOTZARIS 80-20

Telegrammes
LEESONA 93 PARIS

A.B.C. Code
5ᵗʰ Edition

MÉTRO.
LOUIS BLANC

N/ RÉF.

171-173, Quai de Valmy

PARIS (Xᵉ Arrᵗ)

-CERTIFICATE-

We hereby certify that Mr. Dominic MAC CABE has been in our employ from February lst. 1920 to this date, and is leaving us in order to return to England.

During this period, he has had charge of the installation of our machines all over the Continent of Europe up to Greece and Turkey in Asia, and he has thus acquired a great and varied experience. We have also entrusted him with the canvassing of the clientele in these far distant countries and he attended to all the jobs we had confided to him to our full satisfaction.

We, therefore, have pleasure in recommending Mr. MAC CABE as a straightforward and dependable employe, an able mechanic, and a pleasant character. We exceedingly regret his decision to leave our Firm, and wish him every success in the future.

PARIS, March 31st. 1938.

UNIVERSAL WINDING COMPANY.

T.H. RENAUD
Director.

Leaving Certificate from UWC March 31, 1938

Letters and Telegram from Mr R.J. Schilling of Universal Winding Company in Bale to Nick after leaving the company

TELEGRAMS „LEESONA"　　　　　　　　　　　TELEPHON 91505

R. J. SCHILLING
UNIVERSAL WINDING Co. BOSTON (MASS.) U.S.A.
BASEL
DUFOURSTRASSE 40

6th May, 1938

Mr. D. MacCabe,
C/o Westminster Bank,
86, Warton Road,
Brighton, Sussex.

Dear MacCabe,

I wrote you about a week or ten days ago to the above address, but I presume that you have been to your home town, and have in all probability been too busy visiting the wonderful Empire Exhibition at Glasgow to reply earlier.

I want to know particularly under what conditions and how you left the Paris Office, and whether you received anything in the way of a bonus or gratification.

It would have been possible for me to obtain this information by direct methods, but for reasons which may be apparent to you, I did not care to do this. In any case, I have been forced more or less against my will to ask you this, but at the same time I want you to treat this request as strictly private and confidential.

I have my reasons for asking you this, because I have my own personal and private view on this subject, and about which I shall perhaps be more open later on.

As I am leaving here about the 11th or 12th of this month for Turkey and Greece, I would like you to give me your reply as early as possible, and needless to state, anything that you do write will also be treated as a matter only concerning ourselves.

With kindest regards, and hoping that you have been fortunate in obtaining a satisfactory position, I am,

Yours sincerely,

R. J. Schilling (U.W.C. Leesona) Letter May 6, 1938

Charges to pay

s. d.

RECEIVED

No.

OFFICE STAMP

BRIGHTON
5 NOV 39
SUSSEX

98 120 ROADMEN ROTOCONERS +

TELEGRAM

Prefix. Time handed in. Office of Origin and Service Instructions. Words. m

AM2 m

From 78 CCC 1958 4 BASEL 28   To

S A

ELT MACCABE 98 BUCKINGHAM ROAD BRIGHTON :

= HAVE ORDER TEN ROTOCONERS 120 SPINDLES EACH ALEXANDRIA

NO ROADMEN AVAILABLE CAN YOU ACCEPT JOB PROBABLY MIDDLE

FEBRUARY AND WHAT TERMS = SCHILLING +

For free repetition of doubtful words telephone "TELEGRAMS ENQUIRY" or call, with this form
at office of delivery. Other enquiries should be accompanied by this form and, if possible, the envelope.

(U.W.C. Leesona) Telegram November 5, 1939

CABLES "LEESONA"   *Leesona*   TELEPHONE : 3 29 06

R.J. SCHILLING

ST JAKOBSTRASSE 6
BASLE (SWITZERLAND)

REPRESENTING
UNIVERSAL WINDING CO.   BASLE December 15th, 1939
PROVIDENCE RI (U.S.A.)

Mr. D.MacCabe,
98 Buckingham Road,
Brighton (Sussex)
England.

Dear MacCabe,

I duly received your letter of the 5th ulto. and would
ask you to kindly excuse the delay I have taken in answering it.
In the meantime I suppose you have received my letter in which
I gave you full details regarding the proposal I made to you.

Your answer is more or less what I expected, but I
thought that it would give you an opportunity of accepting
it if you happened to be at a loose end. Seeing that you are
now definitely fixed in Brighton, I naturally understand that
you cannot entertain the offer I made, and this need not in
any way cause bad blood between us. To-day more than ever the
slogan is "chacun pour soi".

You will, no doubt, be pleased to learn that the
completion of this order for Misr will be terminated on the
29th December and consignment will be shipped from New York
to Alexandria on January the 6th.

As all our staff at Paris have joined the colours,
I shall be obliged to draw on Manchester, and they have
willingly agreed to help me out. As far as I can see, the
machines should reach Egypt about the end of January or the
first week in February. I have a feeling, however, that the
construction of the mill may have been delayed, and even if
this is not the case, I know that a lot of the preparation
machinery will not be delivered in time.

It will also interest you to know that, apart from
this order for Misr, I have booked orders for Egypt. So we
are now reaping the harvest from the propaganda work I started
some years back in Egypt. Our old friend Willink of Wintswjk
has also opened a knitting factory in Alexandria and has already
placed orders for 2 No.44 machines.

+further   ./.

233

I am very glad to tell you that Mrs.Brun has made a complete recovery and is now out and about again, and she asked me to kindly remember her to you.

With my very best wishes to you all for a very merry Xmas and a more prosperious 1940 I am

Yours sincerely

R.J. Schilling (U.W.C. Leesona) Letter December 15, 1939

1938 and Onwards:
Family in Britain

Jeanne, Ian and Tante Jeanne May 24, 1938

Jeanne and Aunt Dolla at Coldean, Brighton,
August 27, 1955

Tante Jeanne & Jeanne Brighton, June 27, 1963

Tante Cécile and Jeanne in Brighton, April 1963

Theresa, Sheila, Christopher, Andrew Juliet, Jean-Pierre and Jeanne 1967

Jeanne in armchair next to a photo of her grandson Andrew, circa 1983

(9) Letters and Sketches made by Jeanne in her spare time on scraps of paper sometimes sent with her letters to her family.

Letters:

Le 5 September 1966

Dear dear Odette, Jan telephone to day telling me the great news. It is a relief to know you are delivered. my darling. Jan said he is a beautiful baby, a boy. Jan is so happy. I do hope you feel more comfortable now. For a while you'll have to go slowly and for you to get strong. It is always hard for the first baby. I have been thinking of you all the time. I suppose Jan go to see you every evening.

My best congratulations my dear Odette. my tender love.

Your French Maman

X X X X X

Card to Odette September 5, 1966 for the birth of our first son Jean-Pierre.

18/7/1984   J. L Mac Cabe
Loose Valley Private nursing home
Maidstone
Kent

Mes chers enfants.

J' étais si contente de recevoir votre si jolie carte. Portugal doit être un beau pays, cela va vous faire du bien à tous de profiter du beau temps. J' espère que Odette va mieux, et qu' elle s' en donne à coeur vance toi Ian, et que tu profite bien avec vos deux grands fils. Tâcher si vous le pouvez de prendre quelques photos. Le poisson doit être excellent en Portugal, je donnerai je ne sais quoi pour en manger. Ici le poisson n'est mais très frais.

Doug, Sheela et Theresa sont partis

Letter from Jeanne July 18, 1984 – page 1

("Jeanne talks about our holiday in Portugal and says that the fish there must be very good, she would give anything to eat some because where she is the fish is not very fresh!")

le 18 pour les Alpes et espère pouvoir en
voir Yvonne. Ils vont sans doute rester
une quinzaine de jours, profiter de l'a—
et du beau soleil. Ils vont faire des
fréquiniques dans la forêt. Je n'ai pas
encore eu des nouvelles mais Christopher est
venu me donner de leurs nouvelles, Douglas
lui avait Telephoné

Le temps est si beau que nous sommes
restés dans le superbe jardin suivit de
beau chien le "Labrador".

Voilà, mes enfants profitez et
amusez - vous bien et reposez-vous bien
Je vous embrasse bien
fort. Maman ✗✗✗ ✗✗✗✗✗

Letter from Jeanne July 18, 1984 – page 2

("*Jeanne adds that Douglas and his family are going to the Alps and hopes they will see Jeanne's sister, Yvonne. She says the weather is so good that she stays in the superb garden followed by the lovely Labrador dog*")

«Les Croquis» (Sketches) by Jeanne

Peacocks drawn by Jeanne

Geishas by Jeanne

Flowers by Jeanne

More flowers by Jeanne

My parents' Tombstone at Moulescombe, Brighton

Hommage

« *Jeanne,*
Notre Mère,
Dieu t'a donné la beauté, le charme et une nature généreuse,
Toi, tu nous as donné l'amour et le bonheur pendant notre enfance,
Tu nous as apporté une culture et la joie de vivre.
Jeanne,
  Notre Mère,
    Notre Grand-mère,
      Notre amie,
Ton sourire nous a conquis,
Ta bonté nous a touché.
Toujours, nous avons été heureux auprès de toi.
Nous te pleurons aujourd'hui, mais nous garderons pour toujours ton
sourire dans nos pensées.
Que Dieu te récompense par une paix éternelle. »

10) Bibliography

(a) National Archives, Kew
Admiralty Papers
ADM – ADM 53/117020 – HMS Belfast – Ship's Log
Battle Summary BR 1736, N° 24 Sinking of the Scharnhorst
Battle Maps C.B. 3081
Military Operations:
1914–1918 Official War Diaries: Gallipoli – Dardanelles 1915
First quarter 1917 Official War Diaries: La Somme
Military Operations *– Gallipoli – vol. May 2 1915 to the evacuation ed. 1992 (NLS GMM.4/26)*

(b) Books, Articles and Maps
Includes material and research at:
Mitchell Library, Glasgow
National Library of Scotland, Edinburgh
Edinburgh Castle Museum
Registrar Offices in Glasgow and Edinburgh
British Library, London
Imperial War Museum
Brown, Malcolm – La Somme: "Imperial War Museum – Bode of the Somme" Sidgwick and Jackson 1996 (Mitchell Library Glasgow ref: 940.42722.BRO)
Callwell, Major-General Sir Charles Edward Callwell K.C.B.n The Dardanelles, Constable and Co. Ltd., London WC2, 1919
Churchill, Winston – The Gathering Storm Vol 1: The 2nd World War Penguin Books Hammondsworth, Middlesex 1985
Clarke D., G. Mackreth, ODPT – 5th Bn H.L.I. 1914–1918. Canadian Libraries illustr. Col F.L. Morrison (www.pgdp.net) printed for private circulation by Maclehose, Jackson and Co. publisher to the University 1921
Fewster, Kevin, Vecihi Başarın, and Hatice Hürmüz Başarın, Gallipoli, The Turkish Story, Allen and Unwin, Crow's Nest, NSW, Australia, 2003
Henniker, Alan Major: Transportation on the western front, 1914–1918, History of the Great War, ed. 1937 and Maps (National Library of Scotland: NLS GWA.5)

Jenkins, Roy – CHURCHILL – McMillan – Pan Books London 2002

Knox, W.W. "A History of the Scottish People" – Summary of Economy and Society in Scotland 1840–1940, SCRAN – Scotland

Manchester, William: – Winston Churchill – « Rêves de Gloire 1874–1932 » – Édition Robert Laffont, Paris 1985

Manchester. William: – "The Caged Lion" – Winston Spencer Churchill. Michael Joseph, London 1938

Miles, Wilfrid (1885–1962): Military Operations – France and Belgium 1917 – The Battle of Cambrai, ed. 1991 (NLS – GMM. 4/27)

Morrison, F.L. – The Highland Light Infantry 1914–1918, Printed for Private Circulation by MacLehose, Jackson and Co., Publishers to the University in Glasgow, 1921

Murray, Lt Col David – (Queen's Own Cameron Highlanders), Contributed Paper: 52nd HLI. Division at Gallipoli – a Second Flodden:

[1. An edited version of a paper originally published under the title Gallipoli April 1915 – January 1916 in Piping Times. It was submitted to United Service by Colonel Donald Ramsay OAM and edited by David Leece.

Oatts, Lt Col L.B., – "Proud Heritage", The Story of the H.L.I. 1882–1918, ed. Grant

Prior, Robin – Gallipoli – The end of a myth, Yale University Press Newhaven and London – MPG Books Bodmin, Cornwall, 2010

Sheffield, Gary – Forgotten Victory. The First World War – Myths and Realities – Headline Book Publishing REVIEW, 2002

Spears, Major-General Sir Edward – Assignment to Catastrophe – Volume II. The Fall of France June 1940 – William Heinemann Ltd 1954

The Long, Long Trail, The British Army of 1914–1918 – for family historians

www.1914–1918.net/hli.htm

PUNCH Magazines – 1914 and 1915 published at the OFFICE London 1914 and1915

(c) Other Official Documents
Scotland

Census: Glasgow: 1841 – 1851 – 1861 – 1871 –1881 – 1901 – 1911
Various Birth, Marriage and Death Certificates
List of voters in Glasgow
Parish Records

Census 1911, April
Address: 2 Eldon Terrace, Govan, Partick, Glasgow.
Occupants:Dominick McCabe Snr (Spirit salesman)
Mary McCabe (wife)

"Nettie" presumably Bridget (as the age on the census corresponds)
France
"Recensement" (Census) – Nanterre: 1901 – 1911 – Various Birth, Marriage and Death Certificates
Documents of Award to the Mother of Edouard Gastal
Annex: *Additional information obtained from the different Census records.*